Handbook for Ethiopian Public Administration Program Accreditation

Handbook for Ethiopian Public Administration Program Accreditation

Editorial Team
Bacha Kebede Debela (Ethiopian PA Association [EPAA]),
Geert Bouckaert (KU Leuven),
Berhanu Temesgen Eshetu (Addis Ababa University),
Chala Deyessa Fita (Ambo University),
Hailu Megersa Tola (Ambo University),
Kiflie Worku Angaw (KU Leuven),
Shumey Berhie Teshome (Addis Ababa University),
Solomon Gebreyohans Gebru (KU Leuven)

LEUVEN UNIVERSITY PRESS

This book is the second publication within the VLIR project with Project Name: Professionalizing Ethiopian Public Administration to Support Development Practitioners (ET2018JOI007A101)
Web link for the first PA book: https://library.oapen.org/handle/20.500.12657/43000

Published with the support of
VLIR-UOS (Belgium)   KU Leuven   Ambo University

Addis Ababa University   Ethiopian Public Administration Association

Published in 2022 by Leuven University Press / Presses Universitaires de Louvain / Universitaire Pers Leuven. Minderbroedersstraat 4, B-3000 Leuven (Belgium).

Selection and editorial matter © 2022, Bacha Kebede Debela, Geert Bouckaert, Berhanu Temesgen Eshetu, Chala Deyessa Fita, Hailu Megersa Tola, Kiflie Worku Angaw, Shumey Berhie Teshome, Solomon Gebreyohans Gebru
Individual chapters © 2022, The respective authors

This book is published under a Creative Commons Attribution Non-Commercial Non-Derivative 4.0 Licence.

Attribution should include the following information:
Bacha Kebede Debela, Geert Bouckaert, Berhanu Temesgen Eshetu, Chala Deyessa Fita, Hailu Megersa Tola, Kiflie Worku Angaw, Shumey Berhie Teshome, Solomon Gebreyohans Gebru (eds), *Handbook for Ethiopian Public Administration Program Accreditation*. Leuven: Leuven University Press, 2022. (CC BY-NC-ND 4.0)

ISBN 978 94 6270 339 1 (Paperback)
ISBN 978 94 6166 467 9 (ePDF)
ISBN 978 94 6166 468 6 (ePUB)
https://doi.org/10.11116/9789461664679
D/2022/1869/35
NUR: 759
Layout: Crius Group
Cover design: Frederik Danko
Cover illustration: Aranjuez Medina / Vecteezy.com

Table of Contents

List of Abbreviations — 9

Preface — 11

Acknowledgments — 13

About the Editors — 15

Chapter One. The Handbook and Its Structure — 17
    1.1. Introduction to the Handbook — 17
    1.2. The Structure of the Handbook — 19

Chapter Two. International, African, and National Higher Education Contexts — 21
    2.1. International and African Contexts: UN SDG and AU Agenda 2063 — 21
    2.2. Higher Education in Ethiopia: Post-1990s Institutional Context — 22
    2.3. Conclusions — 24

Chapter Three. Public Administration Education in Ethiopia — 25
    3.1. Emperor Haile Selassie's Regime (1930–1974) — 25
    3.2. Derge Regime (1974–1991) — 26
    3.3. BA and Postgraduate Curriculum Development and Review: Post-1991 Ethiopia — 27
        3.3.1. Curriculum Development and Review Process Guiding Principles — 27
        3.3.2. Curriculum Development and Approval Process. — 29
        3.3.3. Procedure for Curriculum Modification — 30
        3.3.4. The Structure of the Curriculum — 32
    3.4. PA Program under the EPRDF Regime — 34
        3.4.1. Bachelor of Arts (BA) (1991–2000) — 34
        3.4.2. Bachelor of Arts (BA) (2000–2013) — 34
        3.4.3. Bachelor (BA) (2013–) — 36

3.5. PA Masters and PhD Programs in Public Universities	38
3.5.1. Master's and PhD Programs PA Curricula	40
3.6. Conclusions	40

Chapter Four. Public Administration Education Accreditation	43
4.1. Why Accreditation?	43
4.2. Elements of Accreditation	45
4.3. Approaches and Types of PA Program Evaluation	46
4.3.1. Approaches to PA Program Evaluation	46
4.3.2. Types of Evaluation: Accreditation versus Audit	48
4.4. Public Administration Education and Training Program Accreditation Institutions	49
4.4.1. International Commission on Accreditation of Public Administration Education and Training Programs (ICAPA)	49
4.4.2. European Association for Public Administration Accreditation (EAPAA)	53
4.4.3. African Higher Education Quality Assurance and Accreditation (AHEQAA)	54
4.4.4. National Association of Schools of Public Affairs and Administration (NASPAA)	57
4.4.5. Other National Experiences: Africa	58
4.5. The Debate on Public Administration Program Accreditation	62
4.6. The Costs and Challenges of Accreditation	64
4.7. Conclusions	65

Chapter Five. Steps to Ethiopian Public Administration Program Accreditation	67
5.1. Beyond De Jure Accreditation	67
5.2. How to Start and Conduct Accreditation?	67
5.3. PA Program Accreditation Initiative in Ethiopia: Lessons from AAU and AU	68
5.4. How to Organize the Accreditation	71
5.5. How to Respond to Recommendations and Use Accreditation as Part of Quality Improvement Strategy?	73
5.6. The Need for Capacity Building to Improve and Sustain PA Program Quality	74

5.7. The Need to Establish an Accreditation Unit and a Network of Ethiopian PA Departments within the Ethiopian Public Administration Association (EPAA): The Proposal	74
5.8. Conclusions	76
Annexes	77
Annex 1. Three PA Curriculums during the Haile Selassie Regime	77
Annex 2. Three PA Curricula during the Derge Regime	79
Annex 3. Three PA Curricula from 1993 to 2000	81
Annex 4. BA in Development Administration Curriculum (ESCU), and BA in PA and Development Management Curriculum (AAU)	83
Annex 5. Harmonized BA Curriculum in Public Administration and Development Management	85
Annex 6. BA Curricula Major in Governance and Development Management/Studies, and BA Major in Development Management	87
Annex 7. MA and PhD Curricula	90
Annex 8. International Commission on Accreditation of Public Administration Education and Training (ICAPA) Self-Assessment Guide Document	97
References	99
Useful Websites	107

List of Abbreviations

AAPAM	African Association of Public Administration and Management
AAU	Addis Ababa University
AFRIQAN	African Quality Assurance Network
AHEQAA	African Higher Education Quality Assurance and Accreditation
APDP	Academic Program Development Office
ASCRC	Academic Standard and Curriculum Review Committee
ASG-QA	African Standards and Guidelines for Quality Assurance in Higher Education
AQRM	African Quality Rating Mechanism
ASRC	Academic Standard and Review Committee
AU	Africa Union
AUC	African Union Commission
AVP	Academic Vice President
BA	Bachelor of Art
DAAD	German Academic Exchange Service
DDS	Democratic Developmental State
EAPAA	European Association for Public Administration Accreditation
ECSU	Ethiopian Civil Service University
ECTS	European Credit Transfer System
EGPA	European Group for Public Administration
ENQA	European Association for Quality Assurance in Higher Education
EPAA	Ethiopian Public Administration Association
EPAN	European Public Administration Network
EPRDF	Ethiopian People's Revolutionary Democratic Front
ESDP	Education Sector Development Plan
EUA	European University Association
FDRE	Federal Democratic Republic of Ethiopia
GTP	Growth and Transformational Plan
HAQAA	Harmonization of African Higher Education Quality Assurance and Accreditation
HEI	Higher Education Institution

HERQA	Higher Education Relevance and Quality Assurance
IASIA	International Association of Schools and Institutes of Administration
ICAPA	International Commission on Accreditation of Public Administration Education and Training Programs
IIAS	International Institute of Administrative Sciences
ISS	Institute of Social Studies
KU Leuven	Catholic University of Leuven
MA	Master of Art
MoE	Ministry of Education
MoFED	Ministry of Finance and Economic Development
MTPA	Management and Public Administration
NAPSIPAG	Network of Asia Pacific Schools and Institutes of Public Administration and Governance
NASPAA	National Association of Schools of Public Affairs and Administration
NISPAcee	Network of Institutes for Public Administration in Central and Eastern Europe
NPC	National Planning Commission
OSU	Oromia State University
PA	Public Administration
PADM	Public Administration and Development Management
PAQAF	Pan-African Quality Assurance and Accreditation Framework
PhD	Doctor of Philosophy
SDG	Sustainable Development Goal
SDPRP	Sustainable Development and Poverty Reduction Program
UN	United Nations
UNDESA	United Nations Department of Economic and Social Affairs

Preface

Improving, assuring, and maintaining the quality and relevance of Public Administration (PA) education and training has attracted increasing attention among PA scholars and practitioners, *international institutions* (such as the International Commission on Accreditation of Public Administration Education and Training Programs [ICAPA]), *regional institutions* (such as the European Association for Public Administration Accreditation [EAPAA]), and *national institutions* (such as the United States' National Association of Schools of Public Affairs and Administration [NASPAA] and the Canadian Association of Programs in Public Administration [CAPPA]). Ensuring the quality and relevance of education, in general, is also the top priority of the United Nations' Agenda 2030, the African Union's Agenda 2063, and of many African governments.

This handbook provides insights on how to improve, assure, and accredit PA education and training programs in Ethiopia. It is consistent with Pan-Africanism and the African Union's Agenda 2063 and contributes to the United Nations Sustainable Development Goals (SDGs), particularly SDGs 4 and 16.

Bizunesh Mideksa Borena
Ambo University

Meheret Ayenew Worota
Addis Ababa University

Acknowledgments

This handbook would not have been possible without the generous support of institutions and individuals. First, we are sincerely indebted to VLIR-UOS (Belgium) for funding two interrelated projects.[1] This handbook is one of the results of a JOINT project. About ten years of funding allowed us to work and network with national and international public administration scholars, establish and support the EPAA, and publish both the first Ethiopian PA handbook and this current handbook, which are landmark contributions to the development of public administration in Ethiopia, and maybe also in Africa. We are also grateful to the project partners for supporting the projects, including the writing of the handbook, and thank the Ethiopian Public Administration Association (EPAA) for its active role in writing the handbook. Who can be against quality and relevance?

Furthermore, we are indebted to many individuals, especially to Martine De Koninck, Ann Hasendonckx, Christel Maes, and Laurens Rademakers (KU Leuven International Office); Annie Hondeghem, Trui Steen, and Marleen Brans (KU Leuven Governance Institute); Steve Troupin (KU Leuven Governance Institute, Project Coordinator); the KU Leuven Public Governance Institute secretariats, particularly to Anneke Heylen (Project Financial Manager), Inge Vermeulen, and Tatjana Van Huyck; and Wannes Verbeeck and Peter Verbeeck (both from VLIR-UOS) for their remarkable support since 2012. We express thanks to Patrick Develtere (KU Leuven) for his systematic support. We sincerely thank all Ethiopian PA scholars for providing us with PA curricula. We are grateful to the Leuven University Press team for preparing this book for publication and to Leuven University Press for publishing this handbook.

Bacha Kebede Debela
Ethiopian Public Administration Association (EPAA)

Geert Bouckaert
KU Leuven

---

1   Namely, the TEAM Project "Strengthening Institutional Capacity to Support Public Administration and or Development Management Programmes at Ambo University," carried out by Ambo University and KU Leuven, and the JOINT project "Professionalizing Ethiopian Public Administration to Support Development Practitioners," carried out by Ambo University, KU Leuven Public Governance Institute (Belgium), and Addis Ababa University.

About the Editors

Bacha Kebede Debela is the President of the Ethiopian Public Administration Association (EPAA). He holds a PhD in Social Sciences from KU Leuven. His main research interest areas include performance management, sustainable development, local government and governance, and developing countries.

Bouckaert Geert is a Professor of Public Management at the KU Leuven, Public Governance Institute, Belgium. He is an Honorary Professor at the Institute for Innovation and Public Purpose of University College London, and Visiting Professor at the University of Potsdam

Berhanu Temesgen Eshetu (PhD) is an Assistant Professor at Addis Ababa University, Department of Public Administration and Development Management (PADM). He is currently serving as Department Head. His research interests include public policy implementation, e-government, public service motivation, and strategic management.

Chala Deyessa Fita is a PhD Candidate at Addis Ababa University and a Lecturer at Ambo University, PADM. His research interest areas are public sector performance and citizen trust in government, institution building, local government, and participant budgeting.

Hailu Megersa Tola is an Assistant Professor of Business Administration at the Department of Management in the College of Business and Economics, Ambo University. His research interest area include leadership and business management.

Kiflie Worku Angaw is a PhD researcher at KU Leuven, Public Governance Institute, and a Lecturer at Dilla University. His main research interests are public administration education and professionalization, policy capacity and civil service system, development policy and public sector institutions, public governance and regional integrations, and ICT in public sectors.

Shumey Berhie Teshome (PhD) is an Assistant Professor of Development Management at Addis Ababa University's Department of PADM. His research interests are development management and governance, aid/development effectiveness, donor coordination, public sector reforms, public policy, and local development.

Solomon Gebreyohans Gebru is a long-serving academic staff member at Mekelle University, Ethiopia, and a PhD researcher at KU Leuven, Public Governance Institute. His PhD research focuses on the governance of higher education systems and institutions. He has published articles on this and other areas.

Chapter One
The Handbook and Its Structure

1.1. Introduction to the Handbook

Both the UN (in Agenda 2030) and the Africa Union (in Agenda 2063) have underlined the increasing importance of inclusive, equitable, quality and relevant education to improve the social well-being and ensure sustainable development (AU 2014a; UN 2015). The devastating Covid-19 pandemic, which has affected all aspects of human development globally (World Bank 2021) and has worsened the prevailing inequalities (World Economic Forum 2020), particularly in Africa (UNECA 2021), has not only exposed the inadequate preparedness of PA and health system (Kuhlmann et al. 2021) but also confirms the need for building a new administrative and governance system (Mascio et al. 2020; Ansell et al. 2021).

The unprecedented challenges demonstrate, among other things, the need to build and strengthen institutions so that they can effectively solve societal problems (Rosenbaum 2015) through, inter alia, ensuring quality and relevance in higher education in all disciplines. To be specific, the recent literature on public administration underlines that research on PA should focus both on knowledge and on improving public administration and public policy (Bouckaert 2020; Ongaro 2020). To this end, the quality and relevance of PA education and research should be assured (Bouckaert & Jann 2020) and PA programs should attract competent students (Bertels et al. 2020).

It is important to note that quality and relevance in PA education and research are crucial for developing countries, particularly in Africa; the continent promotes Pan-African education and research, but most African universities tend to over rely on Western theories for education and research in public administration/management/policy (Debela et al. 2020a; Matsiliza 2020). To address African societal problems, it is imperative that PA education and research should increasingly focus on national and regional development and missions, institutional locations, and the nature of the student population (Newcomer & Allen 2015; Debela et al. 2020a). African scholars should also take into account the sociocultural and economic contexts—including the effect of over sixty years of development aid and the ongoing shift in international development cooperation, namely from the deficit model to the opportunity model, from the plan-centered model to the human-centered model, from the donor-driven model to the mutual win-win model (Develtere et al. 2021)—and increase their research from an African perspective (Crossman 1999; Rugasira 2013) and promote the co-creation and co-production of knowledge.

Additionally, as Rosenbaum (2015) rightly claims, PA academia and practitioners need to understand that strong governments promote change and innovation in the public sector, create enabling conditions for other actors, and have the legitimacy to enforce laws, policies, and rules to solving society's problems. They should also recognize the importance of working to sustain democratic institutions; the need to develop the capacity to function effectively in an environment of rapid change, increasing complexity, and much ambiguity; the increasing need to address issues of poverty and inequality in contemporary society; the necessity to go beyond efficiency and promote public values; the need to significantly increase state capacity; the need to promote cultural, ethnic, and linguistic diversity; and, finally, the necessity to critically observe the ongoing multinational integration and international economic and development cooperation.

Interestingly, in recent years, improving, assuring, and maintaining the quality and relevance of PA education and training has attracted increasing attention among PA scholars and practitioners globally. It has also caught the attention of international institutions such as the UNDESA and ICAPA, regional institutions such as EAPAA, and national institutions such as the United States' NASPAA. Ensuring the quality and relevance of education, in general, is also priority in Agenda 2030 (UN), Agenda 2063 (AU), and African governments. There has also been an increasing trend toward assuring and accrediting the quality and relevance of PA education and training programs, though much remains to be done,, particularly in Africa/Ethiopia and other developing countries.

Drawing on the historical neoinstitutional perspective, a literature review, and document analysis, this handbook, tackles the question: *How has PA education developed in Ethiopia over time and how could the quality and relevance of PA education and training be assured, improved, and maintained?*

1.2. The Structure of the Handbook

The handbook consists of five chapters, including this chapter. Chapter 2 presents the overreaching global and national educational contexts and highlights challenges facing higher education institutions as they seek to ensure equitable access to quality, relevant and inclusive education, and to balance teaching, research, and societal engagement.

Chapter 3 explores and describes the continuities and changes in PA education in Ethiopia since the Haile Selassie regime and reveals how the government's ideology and development programs and policies shape the orientation of PA education in Ethiopia over time. It also points out that much effort is needed to contextualize all BA, MA, and PhD PA programs in Ethiopia.

Chapter 4 explores and describes the international, regional/continental, and national institutions that promote the relevance and quality of PA education and training, assure quality, and provide accreditation. It also highlights the effort undertaken by African nations to harmonize educational curricula and strengthen the quality of higher education institutions and ensure intra-African academic mobility. Further, it demonstrates that the African national quality assurance and accreditation agencies, including the Ethiopian HERQA/ETA, suffer from inadequate institutional capacity.

Chapter 5 explores and describes the benefits and costs of accreditation; the dimensions and types of evaluation; as well as discusses how to organize the accreditation process and respond to recommendations to assure, improve, and maintain the quality and relevance of PA education and training in Ethiopia. The chapter argues that despite monetary and nonmonetary costs and other challenges, the claim for de jure accreditation—which is the case for many universities in Africa and other developing countries and even to some extent in the West—is not sufficient grounds to avoid accreditation in PA education and training. Furthermore, the chapter suggests that institutional capacity building, networking, and establishing a national association of PA schools and networks of PA schools in Africa generally and Ethiopia specifically are essential for promoting the Africanization (Ethiopianization) of public administration education and training. Though the first *Ethiopian PA Handbook* and this handbook contribute to this end, the chapter proposes that the Ethiopian PA and African PA higher education institutions and stakeholders should work diligently toward integrating global and indigenous knowledge to ensure the quality and relevance of PA education and training.

Chapter Two
International, African, and National Higher Education Contexts

2.1. International and African Contexts: UN SDG and AU Agenda 2063

The UN explicitly emphasizes the role of higher education in implementing the seventeen Sustainable Development Goals (SDGs) (UN 2015; Owens 2017; Nhamo & Mjimba 2020). In SDG 4, the UN exclusively focuses on ensuring inclusive, equitable and quality education at all levels of education (UN 2015). The African Union (AU) also put higher education (pan-African education) at the center in the implementation of Agenda 2063 (AU 2014a). AU Goal 2 aims to develop well-educated citizens and a skills revolution underpinned by science, technology, and innovation. Several studies also emphasize the link between sustainable development and higher education (Leal Filho et al. 2015; Finnveden et al. 2019; Albareda-Tiana et al. 2020; Grano & Prieto 2020; Perales Franco & McCowan 2021). Scholars also highlight the need for inclusiveness, effectiveness, and relevance in education and research to generate relevant knowledge and strengthen institutional capacity aimed at solving societal problems (Rosenbaum 2015; Pinheiro et al. 2018; Debela et al. 2020a).

The UN Agenda 2030 and the AU Agenda 2063 set out strong pillars to streamline higher education institutions' towards teaching and research (AU 2014a; UN 2015; Nhamo 2020; Zhou et al. 2020). Agenda 2030 highlights that higher education needs to develop relevant core competencies that fit the seventeen Sustainable Development Goals (SDGs) and connect research with them (Albareda-Tiana et al. 2020; Nhamo & Mjimba 2020; Ketlhoilwe et al. 2020). Among other things, this requires changing the traditional curricula and monodisciplinary teaching and research governance into a relevant interdisciplinary system (Franco et al. 2019; Aleixo et al. 2020; Nhamo & Mjimba 2020; Korhonen-Kurki et al. 2020; Zhou et al. 2020; Ketlhoilwe et al. 2020).

At the same time, Western studies find that higher education institutions do not have adequate institutional capacity and resources to address all SDGs in their education and research and integrate the principles and practice of sustainable development (Fleacă et al. 2018; Albareda-Tiana et al. 2020; Franco et al. 2019; Korhonen-Kurki et al. 2020; Aleixo et al. 2020).

In Agenda 2063, the AU underscores the need to "establish an African Accreditation Agency to develop and monitor educational quality standards across the continent" (AU 2014, 14). The AU seeks to build and expand an African knowledge society through the transformation and investments in universities, science, technology, research, and innovation; and through the harmonization of education standards and mutual recognition of academic and professional qualifications (AU 2014, 14).

Higher education systems in Africa face extraordinary challenges in integrating SDGs and Agenda 2063, including inadequate access to higher education, inequality, insufficient staff competence, and limited access to resources (AU 2014b). The other challenges include disciplinary rigidity, an outdated pedagogical approach, inadequate institutional support, and a poor staff work environment (Zhou et al. 2020). In addition, as the AU (2014b) points out, higher education in Africa fundamentally focuses on teaching with little attention to research. These challenges suggest the need for continued capacity development through partnership across sectors (Owens 2017; Ketlhoilwe et al. 2020). Nevertheless, notwithstanding the difficulties, African higher education and research should use SDGs and AU agenda 2063 as a framework (Useh 2020).

2.2. Higher Education in Ethiopia: Post-1990s Institutional Context

Ethiopia issued a new education and training policy in 1994 (Olkaba 2016; Jiru, 2020). The policy aims to correct shortages in educated and trained human resources, inequitable access to education, inadequate education quality and relevance, inefficiency, and governance problems in the Ethiopian education system (Jiru 2020). It specifies that higher education institutions should be research and problem-oriented and focus on educating students to address societal needs (Federal Democratic Republic Government of Ethiopia 1994). It distinguishes the mother tongue as a language for kindergarten and primary education and English for secondary and higher education. Given that Amharic was the primary school language during Haile Selassie's rule and under the Derge regime, the language shift in primary schools is remarkable. Critical areas of the policy include curriculum and preparation of educational materials; teacher and personnel training and overall professional development; and education institution organization and management reform.

Ethiopia issued five ambitious education sector development plans based on the 1994 education and training policy. The first (1997/98–2001/02) and second (2002/2003–2004/2005) education sector development programs (ESDPs) focused on universal primary education, the expansion of vocational education, and increasing access and equity in education (MoE 1997, 2002; Olkaba 2016). The third and fourth ESDPs (ESDP III &IV) dealt with higher education expansion and quality improvement in general education and emphasized quality and relevance (MoFED 2010; MoE 2010; MoE 2015). ESDP V (2015/16–2019/20) focuses on higher education expansion and quality improvement in the education system (MoE 2015; Olkaba 2016).

Similarly, the four national development plans, from the Sustainable Development and Poverty Reduction Program (SDPRP) (2002–2005) to the Growth and Transformation Plan II (GTP II) (2016–2020) also gave due attention to higher education and capacity building programs (MoFED 2002, 2005, 2010; NPC 2016). The ESPDs and national development plans reinforce the Democratic Developmental State (DDS) ideology and emphasize human resources development, research and networking, and partnership.

However, the focus and the scope of development plans vary. While in the SDPRP and the PASDEP, the government primarily focuses on increasing access and equity in the education sector, in GTP I and GTP 2, the government pays attention to access, quality, and relevance of education (MoFED 2002, 2005, 2010; NPC 2016). Further, the existing plans should be contextualized by the fact that Ethiopia also subscribes to the UN SDGs and the AU Agenda 2063.

In 2010 the government shifted the enrolment ratio into a new student-mix schema (channelling 70 percent of students to the sciences and technology fields and 30 percent into social science and humanities) (MoFED 2010; Olkaba 2016; MoE 2018). However, the 2018 education roadmap introduced a flexible application, revised the 70:30 enrolment policy, and reintroduced a four-year bachelor program (MoE 2018). In 2013 the knowledge-based curriculum was replaced with a competency-based curriculum (MOE 2015). Nonetheless, the competencies are not clearly identified, and the modules and teaching methods are not streamlined (MoE 2018). Besides, the new education roadmap revealed that Ethiopian universities pay little attention to research and community service; they are instead focusing on teaching (MoE 2018).

Despite several capacity-building programs, the quality of education and the institutional capacity of educational institutions in general and of higher education in particular, is inadequate (Tadesse 2014; Debela et al. 2020b; Jiru 2020; Gebru et al. 2020). Furthermore, while there are differences in values and decision-making processes between the indigenous institutions such as the Gada System and the Global democratic system (Gutema 2020), little attempt has been made to harmonize indigenous and global knowledge.

2.3. Conclusions

The UN Agenda 2030 and the AU Agenda 2063 set a framework for implementing the seventeen SDGs and the twenty AU goals (for African universities) for teaching, research, and societal engagement. However, higher education institutions all over the world are struggling to address multiple goals (i.e., teaching, research, and community engagement). We observed that the challenge of integrating all the Agenda 2030 and Agenda 2063 goals would be much higher for African and Ethiopian universities. The thorny issues all over the globe are how to ensure equitable access to quality, relevant, and inclusive education and how to balance teaching, research, and societal engagement. In addition, it may be exceedingly challenging for African universities to harmonize indigenous African knowledge and global knowledge in Pan-African education and research. Higher education institutions can minimize the challenges through continuous capacity building, promoting knowledge co-creation and co-production, and strengthening the respectful partnership of equals.

Chapter Three
Public Administration Education in Ethiopia

3.1. Emperor Haile Selassie's Regime (1930–1974)

In Ethiopia, the BA degree in public administration was first launched in the 1950s at the University College of Addis Ababa, which became Haile Selassie I University in 1961. During this time, an independent Department of Public Administration was established under the Faculty of Arts at Addis Ababa University (AAU 2013; Angaw 2020). During this period, two types of grading systems were in use: numeric and letter. The numeric grading system was used between the 1950s and the early 1960s; subsequently, it was changed to a letter system, ranging from A to F.

Despite some continuities, there were substantial variations between PA curricula between the 1950s and the 1970s. For example, between 1951/52 and 1954/55, the dominant courses in PA curriculum were language, history, economics, philosophy, and law, all of which were taught from a Western perspective. Only two political science courses and one public administration course were included in the program, both of which were Western in origin. Surprisingly, the graduates had taken a biology course that was not related to PA.

However, a shift occurred in the curriculum for the 1960/61 graduates. The number and types of public administration and civil law–related courses were increased. Conversely, languages, history, philosophy, and economics-related courses decreased. Besides, unlike the 1954/55 curriculum, the graduates did take a history of education and biology courses. Interestingly, Development Administration was introduced as part of the subject matter of PA during this period. Here, the role of scholarly debate on building institutions appeared to be significant in shaping the curriculum. In the 1960s, scholars agreed that PA programs should focus on the management of development than the maintenance of law and order (Siffin 2001).

In the continuum, the curriculum for the 1970/71 graduates also changed. Students took more courses related to public administration and social science. The names and numbers of PA courses also significantly differed from those taken by the 1960/61 graduates. The 1970/71 graduates, for instance, took courses related to Ethiopia, which included the Amharic language and Ethiopian Public Administration.

Overall, Haile Selassie's regime intentionally introduced Western courses for two contradictory reasons: to access Western knowledge and to suppress public life and ethnic diversity (Crossman 1999). However, the 1960s saw the emergence of the Ethiopian Student's Movement, which sought the distribution of land to peasants, proclaimed the rights of various ethnic groups, and demanded the equality of nations by raising a fundamental question: Who is an Ethiopian? (Bach 2014; Abbink 2011). All of this led to the overthrow of the regime in 1974. Annex 1 reports the curriculum of three PA cohorts during Haile Selassie's regime.

3.2. Derge Regime (1974–1991)

As in the Haile Selassie regime, AAU remained the only University teaching PA during the Derge regime; the letter grading system similarly remained unchanged. However, PA education drastically changed. First, the PA department lost its independence. Between 1977 and 1981 the program was put under the Department of Political Science and Government (Faculty of Social Sciences) and then under the Department of Management (Faculty of Business Administration) (AAU 2013; Angaw 2020). In 1982 PA was merged with management programs and put under the Department of Management and Public Administration (MTPA) (AAU 2013; Angaw 2020). Second, prior to 1982, when the Derge implemented a mixed economic policy, a socialist-oriented PA program curriculum was developed, based on Marxist-Leninist socialist philosophy. See the PA curriculum between 1976/77–1979/80 in Annex 2.

The PA curriculum between 1982 and early 1990 was composed of socialist and business-related courses; and the program became more interdisciplinary compared to the previous regime. Among other things, the PA program introduced new courses such as research methods and public policy. Third, the merger of the PA and management fields created two graduate streams: a BA major in PA and a BA major in management and public administration (see Annex 2). Fourth, compared to Haile Selassie's regime, the variation of the courses in the program was minimal.

3.3. BA and Postgraduate Curriculum Development and Review: Post-1991 Ethiopia

Since 1991, curriculum development in Ethiopian public universities is guided by the Higher Education Institutions Proclamation and the senate legislation governing universities. The current Higher Education Proclamation sets out that public universities are responsible for developing and implementing relevant curricula and conducting problem-oriented research (FDRE 2019). The legal frameworks also set out that HEIs are responsible for producing internationally competent graduates, promoting and undertaking research that focuses on the needs of the country, ensuring academic freedom and competitiveness, providing relevant community services, ensuring good governance, developing democratic culture, and ensuring stakeholder participation in the governance of the institutions (FDRE 2019). They are also responsible for putting in place appropriate institutional frameworks and mechanisms for curriculum development and its implementation, assessing learning outcomes, developing quality standards, developing reliable internal institutional quality assessment systems, and applying them. As a result, variations between universities' curriculum development processes and university-related legislation are presumed to be small. Benchmarking practices tend to reduce the differences.

3.3.1. Curriculum Development and Review Process Guiding Principles

Every public HEI has the autonomy to "develop and implement relevant curricula and research programs; create new or close existing programs when supported by research and approved by the Minster [in charge of HE] and the Board" (FDRE 2019, Art.16). One of the responsibilities of the Senate, the leading body for academic matters, is "to accredit academic programs with the consensus of the Board and the Ministry (in charge of HE)" (FDRE 2019, Art. 49).

The major guiding principles for curriculum development and review process in Ethiopian HEIs are as follows:
− The curriculum development and review should take into account the mission and educational philosophy of university; national and sectorial development plans and policies; and the economic, social, and politico-administrative context of the country.
− Curriculum development needs to be informed by good practice, nationally and internationally oriented, and take into account the needs of the community.

- Curriculum development should be based on need assessment and adequate analysis of national and regional economic, social and politico-administrative contexts.
- Curriculums should integrate relevant theory and practices and aim at developing the competencies of learners.
- To integrate new development and contexts, curriculums should be reviewed periodically by internal and external relevant stakeholders, including graduating students and alumni.
- The department is responsible for facilitating and organizing a curriculum review based on standards and a specified year. A new curriculum should be reviewed after three cohorts have graduated from the program.
- New curriculum proposals and major modification in the existing curricula shall be approved by the University Senate upon the review and recommendation by the Academic Standard and Curriculum Review Committee (ASCRC)or its equivalent at the university.
- New curricula should be backed by needs assessment and curriculum development workshop reports and approved by responsible academic units (first by departments then by colleges/faculty/school) and sent to the Academic Vice President's Office. Major modification in the existing curricula should also be supported by reports and approved by all responsible units at all levels and sent to the same office.
- The Academic Vice President refers the new curricula and the proposal for major modification to the Academic Program Director or the equivalent office for review.
- The Academic Program Director is responsible for facilitating the meeting of the (ASCRC[2] or its equivalent to discuss and assure the quality and relevance of a curriculum before its endorsement by the University Senate.
- The departments/colleges/faculty/school are responsible for the contents, quality, and effectiveness of the curriculum, as well as for ensuring that the curriculum is student-centred and that the continuous assessment approach is practiced.
- The curriculum must comply with university legislation related to course/modules, credits, and academic level, and to the educational strategies to enhance student's learning outcomes and personal development.
- For undergraduate programs, the curriculum should integrate national compulsory courses.

---

2 The members of the committee range between five to seven and slightly vary between universities. Common to all are the Academic Program Director, Education Quality Assurance and Audit Director, and the University Main Registrar.

- Relevant courses and course contents can be added to nationally harmonized curricula.
- The Educational Quality Assurance and Audit or its equivalent office shall be responsible for assuring the quality and relevance of a curriculum before endorsement by the Senate.
- The Academic Program Development Office or its equivalent is responsible for the registration of all approved curricula all programs of the university.

3.3.2. Curriculum Development and Approval Process.

Despite slight variations between universities, a series of interdependent activities in the curriculum development and approval process include the following:

- The program concept should be initiated at the department level and the initiators should prepare a brief preliminary written proposal consisting of a program description and a rationale for the program and submit it to the department for approval.
- When the program concept is accepted by the department, it shall be submitted to college / faculty / school for approval.
- If a positive response is received at the college / faculty / school level, the program concept shall be submitted to the Academic Vice President's Office, which will be subsequently send to the ASCRC or its equivalent for review and recommendation.
- Following the approval by the Academic Vice President's Office, the colleges /faculties / schools shall start drafting a curriculum for the program.
- Any curriculum development process shall be preceded by a needs assessment, which shall be comprehensive, inclusive, and informed by national and regional development plans and policies, as well as the human resources needs of relevant sectors.
- Program developers shall write the needs assessment report, draft the curriculum, and submit them, together with other supporting documents, to the respective department for review and approval. After programs are approved at the department level, they are submitted to the respective college / faculty / school.
- The college / faculty / school shall refer the draft curriculum and other documents to the college/faculty/school education quality assurance and audit team leader for review and recommendations.

- The college / faculty / school academic commission shall deliberate on the recommended proposal and approve or disapprove the proposed curriculum.
- If the proposed curriculum is adopted from another higher education institution, an internal participatory validation workshop shall be organized upon the approval of the college / faculty / school academic commission.
- If the curriculum is new, upon approval by the college / faculty / school academic commission the proposal shall be submitted to at least two external senior professionals for review.
- The external reviewers shall present written and oral reports at a participatory and inclusive curriculum validation workshop.
- The college / faculty / school shall submit the improved curriculum, report, and the minutes of internal and external validation workshops to Academic Vice President's Office.
- The Academic Vice President shall refer the improved curriculum and all supporting documents to ASCRC or its equivalent for review and recommendation to the Senate through Academic Program Development Director.
- The University Senate shall deliberate on ASCRC's or its equivalent recommendation, make additional remarks if necessary, and make the final decision.
- If the Senate accepts the proposed curriculum and it is "endorsed by the Board and the Ministry of Education (MoE)," the Academic Vice President refers the curriculum to the Academic Program Development Office or its equivalent and to the respective college / faculty / school for promotion, implementation and follow up.

3.3.3. Procedure for Curriculum Modification

The department is responsible for both major and minor modifications to the curriculum.

Major modifications. Major modification includes:
- Any significant change to the objectives and learning outcomes of the program
- Any change to the academic nomenclature of the degree of the academic program
- Changes to the program's total credit hours / ECTC or the relative distribution of credit hours between compulsory and elective courses

- The addition and/or elimination of course(s)
- More than a 50 percent change in the course description and contents of the existing course
- Any change in the credit granted for a module / course
- Any change to course codes / titles or prerequisites
- Any change in the form of instruction or delivery, such as distance or digital learning
- Any change or addition of the location where the program is offered
- Any change in admission requirements

Minor Modifications. Minor modification includes:
- The addition or elimination of a course selection option without changing the relative distribution of elective course credit hours/ECTS
- Any change in the semester breakdown of modules/courses
- Less than a 50 percent change in course description and course contents

Application and Approval
- The department should submit a proposal to modify the curriculum or its components to the college / faculty / school.
- The college / faculty / school should refer the proposal to education quality assurance and to the audit committee for review and recommendations.
- Based on the recommendation of its education quality assurance and audit committee, the college / faculty / school academic commission may approve/reject the modification; in case of approval, it recommends the modification to the Academic Vice President's Office.
- The Academic Vice President shall refer the proposal to ASCRC for review and recommendation.
- Upon the recommendation of ASCRC or its equivalent, major and minor modifications should be respectively approved by the Senate and Academic Vice President.
- The Senate and Academic Vice President shall pass the final decision and the Academic Vice President notifies the decision to the college / faculty / school.
- Nationally harmonized curricula should be approved by the academic commission of each college / faculty / school.
- The college / faculty / school is responsible for the promotion, implementation, and follow-up of the approved curriculum.

3.3.4. The Structure of the Curriculum

Despite slight difference between universities, most educational curricula contain the following key components:

1. Cover Page. The cover page includes the name of the university / college / faculty / school / department, type of program (undergraduate / graduate / postgraduate diploma), name of the program, year.
2. Tables of Contents. Presents the section titles of the curriculum.
3. Background. This section presents the institutional context for the curriculum and introduces its sections.
4. Rationale This section clearly explains the relevance of the program. The justification should be supported by the needs assessment report, the importance of the program for national, regional, and local economic, social, and political development, and the expected job opportunities available to the program graduates. The section should also show how the program contributes to the university mission and goals.
5. Learning Outcomes. This section specifies the general expected learning outcomes of the program graduates.
6. Professional Profile. In this section the curriculum describes the expected professional profile of graduates. It describes the type of professional occupation the graduate can work in.
7. Graduate Profile/Competencies. This section lists the overall competencies (knowledge, attitude, and skills) of the program graduates.
8. Entry / Admission Requirement. Based on university legislation, national policy frameworks, and the nature of the program, the curriculum should clearly specify the program entry requirements.
9. Duration of the Program. This section specifies the number of years and semesters needed to complete the program for each mode of delivery (regular, extension, summer, and distance).
10. Graduation Requirement. In general, the graduation requirement shall be in line with university legislation. Specific requirements may be briefly added in this section.
11. Degree Nomenclature: In this section the curriculum should correctly specify the name of the degree as it appears in the diploma of the program graduate, in English and Amharic.
12. Mode of Delivery. These include the semester system, block system, or a combination of these, delivered face to face, by distance, via digital learning, etc.
13. Teaching learning approach. This section provides the general overview of instructional philosophy, major teaching –learning methods

14. Assessment and Evaluation Mechanisms. Taking into account the individual university's legislation, here the curriculum is expected to clearly indicate the assessment philosophy and approach.
15. Grading System: This section outlines the grading thresholds and corresponding letter grades.
16. Human Resources and Infrastructures. This section describes available resources (human and nonhuman) and other required resources, including infrastructures and materials.
17. Quality Assurance mechanism. This section specifies quality assurance techniques, measurement, and assessment strategies.
18. List of Modules / Courses and Codes. This section presents a list of modules and / or courses and their codes.
19. Module / Course Breakdown. This section presents the module/course breakdown for each semester based on provisions in the university's legislation and a logical module/course sequence.
20. Course Guidebook. The course guidebook is expected to contain the following.
    – Name of the university, college / faculty / school / department
    – Name of program
    – Course title
    – Course code
    – Module name and number
    – ECTS / credit hours
    – Study hours per week for modular curricula
    – Target group
    – Year / semester
    – Prerequisite
    – Course description
    – Course objectives
    – Course contents
    – Teaching-learning method
    – Assessment mechanisms
    – Course polices (e.g., attendance, project work, individual / group assignment)
    – List of references

3.4. PA Program under the EPRDF Regime

3.4.1. Bachelor of Arts (BA) (1991–2000)

After toppling the Derg regime in 1991, the Ethiopian People's Revolutionary Democratic Front (EPRDF) established the Transitional Government of Ethiopia (with fourteen regional governments [1991–1995]) and the Federal Democratic Republic of Ethiopia (with nine regional states and two city administrations) in 1995 (Peterson 2015; Debela et al. 2020a). Nevertheless, the politico-administrative reform did not change the PA curriculum that had existed during the last years of the Derg regime. The PA program from 1991 to 2000 included public administration and business administration courses that were almost identical with those of 1989/90 graduates who majored in PA (see Annex 3). The difference between the curricula was less than 10 percent, indicating minor modification in the curriculum while revealing the path dependency. This is partly because, during this period, the country officially embraced elements of neo-liberal ideology (Mengesha & Common 2007; Peterson 2015; Debela & Troupin2020), while the regime in power promoted the Marxist-Leninist inclined revolutionary democracy. This latter had been reinforced since the struggle period against the Derge regime, which was also a socialist government (Hagmann & Abbink 2011; Bach 2011; Vaughan 2011; Aalen 2020). The program retrieved some courses from the curriculum as it stood under Haile Selassie's regime. Noteworthy is that the PA program introduced a computer course during this period.

3.4.2. Bachelor of Arts (BA) (2000–2013)

During this period, drastic changes were imposed on the PA program. First, the institutional independence of the PA program was restored, after nearly three decades. An independent Department of Public Administration and Development Management was established within the Faculty of Business and Economics, at AAU, in 2004 (AAU 2013). Second, the new institutional arrangement also changed the nomenclature of the BA program to BA Major in Public Administration and Development Management, which created a fertile ground for the rapid spreading of similar PA program in other public universities following the massive public university expansion that began in the 2000s. Third, a four-year bachelor's PA program was reduced to a three-year program in the 2003/2004 academic year, assuming a one-year university education in high schools. As a result, unlike the previous periods in which all students in a cluster (for example, in social sciences), were required to take common courses before being placed in colleges and then departments based on their first-year academic grade and preferences, this period was marked by direct admission to the relevant faculty / college. Placement in the department was competitive for all programs, but female students had priority.

Fourth, in 2007 and 2009, Hawassa University and Jimma University, respectively introduced a new and highly PA-related BA program entitled the "BA in Governance and Development Studies," (Hawassa Universality 2013). Indeed, the Ethiopian Civil Service University (ESCU) (since 1996) and Ambo University (since 2006) have been teaching a three-year BA program in Development Administration/Management. Currently, fourteen public PA universities teach BA programs in Public Administration and Development Management, and six universities offer BA programs in Development Management / Governance and Development Studies / Governance and Development Management (See Table 1).

Except at Mekelle University, where Public Administration and Development Management is under the Department of Marketing, the BA program in Public Administration and Development Management has an independent department— the Department of Public Administration and Development Management within the College of Business and Economics. Except for ECSU, the Governance and Development Management program and related nomenclature have independent departments located in different institutions. At Ambo, Bahir Dar, Hawassa, and Jimma Universities, the program is managed by the Department of Governance and Development Management Studies under the College / School of Law and Governance; at Wolkite University, it is managed by the Department of Governance and Development Studies under the College of Social Science and Humanities. At ECSU, the program is under the Department of Economics and Management and embedded under the College of Finance, Management, and Development.

Table 1. List of Ethiopian Public Universities Offering PA / PA-Related Programs (2021–)

List of Universities	Name of the Program
Addis Ababa, Ambo, Asossa, Haramaya, Dire Dawa, Gambella, Jijiga, Dilla, Mekelle, Wachemo, Wolaita Sodo, and Wollega, University of Gondor	Public Administration and Development Management
Ambo, Bahir Dar, Hawasa, Jimma, ECSU, and Wolkite	Development Management / Governance and Development Studies / Governance and Development Management

ECSU and Oromia State University (OSU), the public sector–focused Ethiopian PA universities whose targets are civil servants, are teaching other specialized BA programs in the PA field. The former, for example, teaches a BA in Public Finance Management and a BA in Public Procurement and Asset Management, while OSU, the only regional university, offers a BA in Human Resource Management and Leadership and other related programs. They work respectively with the federal and regional institutions responsible for the management of civil servants and provide training to civil servants. Of course, the Ethiopian Management Institute, Regional Leadership Academies, and other universities also train civil servants.

The expansion of PA programs was, among other factors, stimulated by benchmarking experiences, namely: the Ethio-Eritrean war (1989–2000) that systematically triggered the introduction of the second phase and a district-level decentralization in 2001 (World Bank 2013; Peterson, 2015); the surge and regionalization of universities since the 2000s; and policy learning from the results of national development programs and sectoral development plans.

Due to benchmarking, the difference between the BA program in Development Administration (ECSU) and the BA program in Public Administration and Development Management (AAU) was minor, with the former comprising more generic development and law-related courses, and the latter program focusing on local government and public sector courses (see Annex 4). Except for two courses, the BA curricula in Public Administration and Development Management for 2000/01–2004/05 and 2004/05–2008/09 years were almost identical.

However, between 1990 and 2000, there were revisions to the PA program, including the removal of comparative and socialist-oriented courses. Instead, the program introduced new courses such as Civic and Ethical Education, Entrepreneurship, and Introduction to Demography. Interestingly, after four decades, the program reintroduced the Development Administration course.

3.4.3. Bachelor (BA) (2013–)

BA Major in Public Administration and Development Management
Ethiopian public higher education institutions harmonized and modularized their BA/BSc educational curricula nationally in 2012. The universities started implementation in the 2013/2014 academic year. The universities also changed their grading system from criteria-based to point reference. ECSU and OSU were exceptions; they modularized their curricula but did not nationally harmonize them. As a result, despite the universities having space

to add course contents and introduce other relevant courses, the bachelor's program\s are standardized in all public universities. In addition, the HEIs, including ESCU and OSU, adopted the European Credit Transfer System (ECTS). The argument was that the harmonization and modularization of education curricula and a uniform grading system ensure the quality and relevance of education and the comparability of the programs, and reduce the challenges in handling student transfer cases between Ethiopian universities.

The new shift appeared to parallel the Ethiopian government's interest in reinforcing the Democratic Developmental State (DDS) doctrine the country officially adopted after the 2005 relatively free but contested national election (Abbink 2006; Vaughan & Gebremichael 2011; Lefort 2012; Clapham 2018). Since 2005 the EPEDF has officially reinforced DDS doctrine driven by "developmental capitalism" and "democratic centralism." Consequently, the federal parliament was transformed into a single-party parliament in the 2015 national election (Debela et al. 2020a); subsequently, the country was rocked by mass protests between 2015 and 2018, laying the ground for the coming into power of Prime Minister Abiy Ahmed in 2018.

Between 2000 and 2013, the harmonized and modularized Bachelor's in Public Administration and Development Management curriculum retained the majority of PA courses offered by the AAU. The new curriculum introduced four new and removed four existing courses (see courses with "+" sign in Annex 5). It appears that the scope of some courses increased. Examples of such courses are: Introduction to Public and Development Administration and Public Sector Financial Administration.

Following the adoption of the 2018 education roadmap and the reintroduction of a four-year bachelor program (MoE 2018), the BA curriculum in Administration and Development Management was harmonized for the second time in 2020, and its implementation has started in the 2020/21 academic year. The new curriculum has maintained all courses from 2013–2020, but the scopes of five courses has increased and a few other courses have slightly modified their names (see courses with "*" in Annex 5). The curriculum (re)introduced fifteen new courses, of which nine are fundamentally unique to the Ethiopian BA PA program (see courses at the bottom of the Annex 5). Overall, the new curriculum tends to develop students' competencies to contribute to SDGs, the AU Agenda 2063, and the ongoing national political-administrative reforms.

BA Major in Governance and Development Management / Studies
Similar to the BA program in Public Administration and Development Management, the BA curriculum program in Governance and Development Studies and/or Development Management has changed. Between 2007 and 2012, nine

courses were removed from the curriculum to develop the 2013 nationally harmonized curriculum. Instead, nine new courses were introduced (see the removed courses at the bottom of Annex 6). The harmonization also slightly changed the names and scope of seven courses (see the courses in italics).

The four-year harmonized BA curriculum (2020/21) introduced fourteen new courses, eight of which are identical with courses in the BA program in Public Administration and Development Management (2020/21). In addition, these BA programs have fourteen similar courses, of which the majority are core courses.

Interestingly, the nonharmonized BA curriculum in Development Management at the ECSU has nineteen courses similar or closely identical to the harmonized BA programs in Governance and Development Studies, and Public Administration and Development Management. Annex 6 presents four BA curricula in Governance and Development Management / Studies and Development Management.

3.5. PA Masters and PhD Programs in Public Universities

Public administration education at the masters and PhD levels were launched at AAU respectively in 2005 and 2010, indicating the university is also a trendsetter for postgraduate programs. Currently, ten public universities offer a two-year master's program in different specializations in regular and extension programs; three of them also offer a four-year PhD in the regular program (Table 2).

The major stimuli for the launching of and the increase in the number of masters and PhD programs in PA are related but sequential. First, in 1996 AAU, in collaboration with the Institute of Social Studies (ISS), the Netherlands, started a master's program in Regional and Local Development Studies. The capacity building component of the project allowed the AAU staff to obtain their PhDs, which not only strengthened the institutional capacity of the program but also created an opportunity for the launching of a Master's of Arts in Public Administration in 2005 in the Faculty of Business and Economics, Department of Public Administration and Development Management.

The second important factor for the surge in postgraduate programs is the massive expansion of BA and MA PA and related programs and the parallel demand for qualified academic staff (AAU 2010, 2012). The third crucial rationale for the progression in postgraduate studies is the increasing demand for highly qualified human resources in the public sector (see, for example, ECSU 2017; ESCU 2018, 2019). Finally, this phenomenon can also be explained by the competition between universities.

However, it should be noted that the overwhelming majority of Ethiopian PA scholars have no PhD (Angaw 2020) and many Ethiopian public universities rely on expatriates for postgraduate programs. This does not only limit the contextualization of teaching and research but also endangers the quality and sustainability of the programs.

Table 2. List of MA and PhD PA Universities and the PA Programs

List of PA Universities	Name of Master's and PhD Program
AAU (2[3]), Asossa, Bahir Dar, Dire Dawa (2[4]), ECSU, Jimma, Wollega and Hawasaa	Master's in Public Management and Policy (AAU & DDU) / Public Administration (Assosa and Wollega) / Public Management and Governance / (Barhir Dar), Public Management (ECSU and Jimma), Public management and Policy development (Hawassa)
Ambo, Bahir Dar, ECSU, Hawasa (3[5]), Jimma (2[6]), and OSU	Master's in Development Management / Governance & Development / Public Management and Policy Development
ECSU (4)	Master's in Public Policy Studies, Development Policy, Policy Analysis, and Social Policy
ECSU (3)	Master's in Peace and security, Social Security Management, and Migration and Development
ECSU (3)	Master's in Public Procurement and Asset Management, Tax Administration and Tax Custom Administration
OSU	Master's in Leadership and Change Management
ECSU	Master's in Leadership and Good Governance
ECSU, and OSU	Master's in Public Financial Management
AAU	PhD in Public Management and Policy
AAU	PhD in Federal Studies
AAU	PhD in Peace and Security
ECSU	PhD in Public Management
ECSU	PhD in Public Finance Management
Hawassa	PhD in Policy and Development Studies

3 Development Management, and Public Policy and Governance
4 Development Management, Public Policy and Governance
5 Governance and Development, Development Management, and Public Management and Policy Development
6 Governance, and Development Management

3.5.1. Master's and PhD Programs PA Curricula

The MA and PhD curricula are diverse but share some features. Both MA and PhD programs have courses on public policy, advanced research methodology courses, and a thesis (Master's and PhD dissertation, respectively) is required for graduation. The PhD program offers course-based training for one year and appears to be theory-driven, as the students may not have enough time to write both papers and a PhD dissertation. Indeed, in practice, Ethiopian master's programs are also theory-driven, affecting practice-oriented teaching and research.

However, there are variations between programs and universities in terms of the scope and focus. For instance, some policy courses are generic while others are specific. Compared to other PA universities, the master's and PhD programs at ECSU tend to be predominantly public sector-oriented and specific. The MA programs at OSU are also policy oriented. This should not come as a surprise, as ECSU and OSU are officially responsible for strengthening public sector institutions' capacity to implement development plans and policies.

The PA master's programs may be classified into five clusters: (1) Public Administration/Management, (2) Development and Public Policy, (3) Public Financial Management, (4) Leadership and Governance, and (5) Development Management and Governance. The curricula of twenty master's and five PhD programs provide interesting insights on the nature and focus of PA programs (see annex 7)

3.6. Conclusions

Drawing on the historical neoinstitutionalist perspective and an analysis of PA curricula over time, this chapter examined the continuities and changes in PA education in Ethiopia. Four conclusions are noteworthy. First, we saw that PA education in the country began at Addis Ababa University in the 1950s and has been diffusing to other universities since the mid-2000s. This holds for BA, MA, and PhD programs, but MA and PhD training began more recently than the BA: the MA since 2005 and the PhD since 2010. Currently, twenty Ethiopian universities are teaching PA. Second, we observed that, during the Haile Selassie and Derge regimes the institutional embeddedness of the PA program at AAU was unstable. Except at Mekelle University, an independent PA department has been in charge of PA programs since 2005; that department is hosted either under the College/Faculty of Business and

Economics (the majority), College/School of Law and Governance, and College of Social Science and Humanities.

Third, we noticed that PA education in Ethiopia has moved from disciplinary fragmentation during the Haile Selassie regime to a relatively stable interdisciplinary field launched during the last years of the Derge regime and further consolidated since the 1990s. Since 2013, national harmonization and modularization based on lesson from the Bologna process has significantly contributed to the standardization of BA PA programs in Ethiopia. However, the harmonization and modularization initiatives have not reversed the majority of PA program courses. The role of a benchmarking practice also appears to be significant. The MA and PhD programs are diverse but share some features: they teach public policy-oriented and research methodology courses, and a master's thesis or PhD dissertation are required for graduation. Overall, although the extent of the contextualization of the course syllabus is hard to ascertain, the number of Ethiopian PA courses was low for all BA, MA, and PhD PA programs.

Last but not least, Ethiopia's public higher education proclamations and university legislation guide the curriculum and review process. The similarity of the guiding principles and experience sharing tend to reduce the difference between universities in terms of the structure of the curricula. Interestingly, government/regime ideology and the government's development programs and policies tend to shape the orientation of PA education in Ethiopia: feudalism (under Haile Selassie), socialism (under the Derge), Developmental State/state capitalism (under the EPRDF). The Prosperity Party–led government has expounded *Medemer* (meaning "synergy") rhetoric. Whether this will be the regime's ideology is yet to be seen.

Chapter Four
Public Administration Education Accreditation

4.1. Why Accreditation?

Historically higher education accreditation emerged after World War II in the United States, when independent, self-governing, external review entities called accreditors were institutionalized to assure the quality of higher education (McFarland 2015).

The literature distinguishes two types of higher education accreditation: institutional-level and program-level. Higher education institutions can seek both institutional and program accreditations (Katsamunska 2015). Katsamunska (2015) maintains that institutional accreditation focuses the assessment and the accreditation of higher education based on the extent to which the organization achieves its mission and objectives and the strength and effectiveness of institutional arrangement (policies and procedures) and management practices meant to ensure internal institutional quality and effective partnership management with other higher education and other institutions. Institutional accreditation implies that the institution has adequate capacity and "effective quality assurance mechanisms for its program" (van der Krogt 2015, 104). Program accreditation, on the other hand, focuses on the quality of the program, and the assessment criteria are program-focused (Katsamunska 2015; van der Krogt 2015).

The extant literature widely discusses the benefits of accreditation. Hayward (2006, 8) points out that institutional and program accreditation and quality audits serve a wide range of purposes, including:
- assessing the performance of tertiary institutions, including teaching, learning, research, and service;
- improving the quality of higher education, which in many cases means meeting international standards and expectations;
- protecting the public from fraudulent or substandard tertiary education providers;
- providing institutions with an external assessment of quality and performance and encouraging quality improvement;

- providing information to potential students, their parents, employers, and the public;
- assessing the relevance of academic and professional programs;
- providing for licensure in professional fields;
- setting minimum standards for higher education institutions (in the case of accreditation);
- examining quality improvement and institutional assessment mechanisms;
- assessing the success of institutions in meeting their stated missions, goals, and vision;
- holding tertiary institutions accountable to the public and stakeholders;
- providing mechanisms for government regulation of higher education;
- assisting governments in allocating resources;
- protecting the integrity of the meaning of higher education terminology, including "university," "college," "professor," "dean," and related terms as a public good, from misuse and misapplication; and
- providing a recognized measure of quality to attract foreign students and investors, ensuring the transferability of students and recognition of student degrees internationally.

Rosenbaum (2015) distinguishes three benefits of PA education and training program accreditation. First, he notes that PA quality criteria and standards stimulate self-assessment and reflection thereon helps to improve the quality and the relevance of the program. Second, he asserts that PA education and training program accreditation enables institutions, departments, and programs to obtain the needed human and nonhuman resources. At the very least, it increases attention and a modest investment in the program. Third, he maintains that accreditation provides an excellent opportunity to identify priorities for future program development and foster the development of PA education and training. Accreditation could serve as testimony of the quality and relevance of the program. Similarly, Daemen and van der Krogt (2008) identify four functions of accreditation:

1. *Accountability function*. Accreditation testifies that the institution or the program maintains adequate accountability and compliance with international standards, the national education system, and policies. The accountability function enables the organization to inform citizens/customers and societal actors that the institution upholds adequate accountability in addressing public interest, which is particularly important for publicly funded HEIs that rely on the government's budget. The government is responsible for ensuring the accountability of HEIs for the

use, misuse, and abuse of public resources. Ideally, accredited programs are more legitimate in terms of their claim for public funding than their counterparts.
2. ***Quality assurance function***. Accreditation enables the institution and the department to stimulate and maintain the quality of programs. The self-assessment, the site visit, and the accreditation process provide a strong stimulus for dialogue, and the internal and external quality assurance help maintain the quality of the program (Pattyn et al. 2008). To this end, the accreditation system, among other things, should present reliable and valid information on the content of the program, the balance between theory and practice, the pedagogical structure of the program, and the structure and quality maintenance culture. Ideally, if the program is internationally accredited, the graduates receive an internationally recognized diploma.
3. ***Disciplinary function***. Accreditation safeguards the identity and integrity of the discipline of public administration. This is crucial because PA is an interdisciplinary or multidisciplinary field, and the diversity of PA programs leads to different interpretations of the discipline.
4. ***Emancipatory function***. Accreditation ensures the development of PA as an independent field of study. International/national accreditation ensures the comparability of PA program quality that allows for staff, student, and graduate mobility. A peer-review process and international accreditation significantly contribute to the development of the PA field (Klun & Reichard 2019).

4.2. Elements of Accreditation

Van der Krogt (2015) distinguishes four elements of accreditation. Defining a set of criteria and standards is the first element. For van der Krogt (2015), while criteria refer to sets of yardsticks/checkpoints/benchmarks against which the attainment of objectives can be examined, standards are the expected level of requirements (thresholds) against which the quality of higher education and their programs are assessed to offer accreditation or certification by the accrediting agency. Criteria and standards can be imposed by government, national/ regional, or international organization, but mission-based evaluation helps to integrate organizational criteria and standards. Brintnall (2015) maintains that international standards enable effective investment (resource allocation) in PA programs, improve and maintain the quality of the program, institutionalize inclusiveness and core values in the PA program, and ensure PA program consistency in all institutions.

The second crucial element in the accreditation process is the *sources of information* used, which predominantly comprise a self-evaluation report and a site visit by external evaluators. The third element concerns the *judgment process* for the final accreditation decision. The last step is a *follow-up* to the decision comprising either improvement or termination of the program. The former involves evaluating the accreditation process, monitoring improvement plans, monitoring improvement activities, and monitoring the effects of the improvement (van der Krogt 2015).

4.3. Approaches and Types of PA Program Evaluation

4.3.1. Approaches to PA Program Evaluation

There are different approaches to PA program evaluation. For example, van der Krogt (2015) identifies the following eight dimensions to evaluating PA education and training programs, which could be used in any country:

Internal versus external evaluation: This model is based on who performs the evaluation and the purpose of the evaluation. While internal evaluation is done by the organization itself, external evaluation is performed by an external evaluation/accreditation agency, which is presumed to be independent. Among others the purposes of internal evaluations are: (1) the safeguarding of institutional or organizational standards; (2) improvement and enhancement of quality; and (3) fulfilment of external demands (via external evaluation). Internal evaluation is internally initiated and is a prerequisite for external evaluation.

Van der Krogt identifies five purposes of evaluation: (1) the safeguarding of national academic standards for higher education; (2) ensuring accreditation of programs and/or institutions; (3) safeguarding consumer, client, or user protection; (4) providing independent (quantitative and qualitative) information to the public about the programs or institutions; and (5) improving and enhancing the quality of a program. Both types of PA program evaluation reinforce each other. If performed objectively, comprehensively, and periodically, both improve and maintain the quality of the PA program.

Formative versus summative evaluation: This model concerns who make the judgment and decides the purpose of evaluation. For van der Krogt (2015), *formative* evaluation focuses on how to improve the quality and relevance of the institutions or program and experts pass the judgment and provide recommendations; alternatively, the purpose of *summative* evaluation is accreditation and the judgment lies in the hands of peers and the accreditation agency. Hence, summative evaluation contributes to the fulfillment of accountability, quality assurance, disciplinary, and emancipatory functions.

Institutions versus Programs evaluation: This model concerns the object of evaluation. While institutional (the object) evaluation targets institutional accreditation as a whole, program evaluation focuses on assessing the quality of the program and program accreditation (Hayward 2006; van der Krogt 2015). The latter is increasingly common for PA education and training programs.

Peer versus non-peer evaluation: This model is based on who conducts the evaluation. For van der Krogt (2015), peer (professionals in the field) evaluation is used if the objective of the assessment is program improvement (formative evaluation). For accreditation (final judgment), since it could be difficult for peers to be sufficiently objective, the evaluation team or site visit team should be composed of peers from another country and representatives of practitioners, students, and/or alumni (van der Krogt 2015).

Evaluation of internal efficacy versus evaluation of external efficacy: This approach is based on the frame of reference for evaluation and use. Whereas evaluation of external efficacy seeks to meet the requirements of external agents (external comparison and judgment), evaluation for internal efficacy focuses on comparing the program against internal objectives and aims at internal use (van der Krogt 2015)

Mission-based versus "normal" evaluation: This model is based on the reference point of the standards. Standards for normal evaluation are structured and defined by external or internal authorities. Mission-based evaluation is based on the mission of the program. It relies on semi-structured standards, comprising externally and internally defined criteria and standards (van der Krogt 2015). The International Commission on Accreditation of Public Administration Education and Training Programs (ICAPA), the European Association for Public Administration Accreditation (EAPAA), and the National Association of Schools of Public Affairs and Administration (NASPAA) uses the mission-based evaluation. Section 4.3 provides details on these institutions.

Voluntary versus mandatory evaluation: This model is based on the consequence of evaluation. Mandatory evaluation (accreditation) implies the institution and/or the program should be evaluated (accredited) to get a license to teach a program and provide a diploma and/or a degree (van der Krogt 2015). This is often the case for private HEIs in Ethiopia. Though a license is mandatory for the institution or the program, voluntary evaluation is sought by institutions or programs to assure their quality (van der Krogt, 2015). The ICAPA, NASPAA, and EAPAA are based on a voluntary system.

Degree (BA, Master's, and PhD) versus non-degree level program evaluation: This approach is based on the level of the academic program. According to van der Krogt (2015), bachelor level evaluation strongly emphasizes the quality and relevance of the curriculum and the organizational aspect; the master's level evaluation targets specific program content and learning outcomes; and the PhD level evolution focuses on the extent to which the program fosters a research-driven learning environment. A non-degree training program evaluation might have its own approach (van der Krogt 2015). Until now, only ICAPA offers accreditation for BA, master's, PhD, and non-degree training programs all over the world.

Academic level versus professional competence evaluation: This model is based on whether the academic level or an individual is evaluated. While academic level evaluation focuses on the quality of graduates' academic level (bachelor, master's, or doctoral), professional evaluation pays attention to professional level competencies, often backed by professional license and certification to practice in the field (van der Krogt 2015). However, it should be noted that the high quality of graduates' academic level may not correlate with professional-level competencies.

4.3.2. Types of Evaluation: Accreditation versus Audit

Van der Krogt (2015) points out that accreditation and audit are the most common types of evaluation. For him, these types are conceptually related and apply a similar approach, but their purposes are slightly different (see also Hayward 2006). Both rely on criteria and standards and apply similar methods (self-evaluation, site visit, reporting, and judgment). But they are also different. Audit focuses on how well the institution or the program properly functions to meet its objectives. Contrarily, accreditation seeks to identify to what extent the institution or program proves its worthiness (van der Krogt 2015). Second, audit complements internal quality assurance and is relevant for long-established higher education institutions and programs, and accreditation is more crucial for new institutions and programs. However, following the Bologna process, accreditation is becoming popular in many European countries and is sought even by long-established HEIs and programs.

4.4. Public Administration Education and Training Program Accreditation Institutions

4.4.1. International Commission on Accreditation of Public Administration Education and Training Programs (ICAPA)

The establishment of the International Institute of Administrative Sciences (IIAS) in 1930, in Brussels, was the landmark event for the promotion and development of administrative sciences worldwide (Mishra 2015; Rosenbaum 2015). Remarkably, in 1960, IIAS members meeting in Lisbon established the International Association of Schools and Institutes of Administration (IASIA) to "promote excellence in public administration education and training" (Rosenbaum 2015, 17). At the 1998 annual conference in Paris, IASIA critically deliberated on the accreditation agenda and initiated a worldwide accreditation process. Subsequently, in 2005, the United Nations Division of Public Administration and Development (UNDESA) and IASIA Joint Task Force was established to work on Standards of Excellence for Public Administration Education and Training. The taskforce developed eight developmental and aspirational Standards of Excellence for IASIA to guide the development and assess the quality of PA programs, which were accepted by UNDEA and IASIA in 2009. Each standard has sub-standards. After three years (i.e., in 2012) IASIA agreed to assess and accredit PA education and training programs internationally and established the International Commission on Accreditation of Public Administration Education and Training Programs (ICAPA), in 2013; it began accreditation in 2014 (Rosenbaum 2015).

ICAPA accredits bachelor, master's, and PhD programs, as well as training programs in the field of public administration (Rosenbaum 2015). It does not accredit institutions. The object of accreditation is the public administration program that the organization offers (van der Krogt 2015). ICAPA has so far accredited two BA,[7] six MA,[8] one PhD,[9] and one non-degree programs[10] (https://iias-iisa.org/page/icapa-accreditated [accessed on 14 April 2022]).

ICAPA sees its mandate as including three types of activities: advice, rostering, and accreditation (Rosenbaum 2015). When the program is at the initial stage, ICAPA provides advice on how to develop the program and enhance its quality. If the program is of outstanding quality but not fully matured for formal accreditation, ICAPA puts it on the rostered program. If the program is fully matured, ICAPA will conduct a full assessment for accreditation, with two outcomes: accreditation or denial. The latter may be subjected to written appeal to ICAPA for a final judgment (Rosenbaum 2015). ICAPA uses a peer-based evaluation system. The ICAPA accreditation process involves four steps (Rosenbaum 2015):

A. **Self-Evaluation.** The applicant needs to conduct an extensive self-assessment based on the self-assessment guide (see Annex 8 for brief contents) and submit the report to ICAPA. Upon initial review of the self-assessment report, ICAPA can request additional documents.
B. **Site visit.** ICAPA appoints a team of four individuals (one a member of ICAPA, one practitioner/student selected by ICAPA; the remaining two are PA scholars) to conduct a site visit for two to five days. The timing for the site visit depends on the agreement between the team and the requesting institution. The site visit team needs to conduct an exit interview to complement the field information.
C. **Reporting.** The ICAPA team evaluates the program against UN / IASIA Standards of Excellence for Public Administration Education and Training and is expected to present a comprehensive report to ICAPA.

---

7   Ghent University, Belgium (Bachelor of Science in Public Administration and Management Program, 2019), Universidad Externado de Colombia, Colombia (Bachelor's in Government and International Relations, 2019).
8   Escola Brasileira de Administração Pública e de Empresas de Riode Janeiro – Fundacão Getúlio Vargas, Brazil (Master of Public Administration Program, 2014), School of Public Affairs and Administration at Rutgers University – Newark, United States (Master of Public Administration Program, 2015), American University in Cairo, Egypt (Master of Public Policy Program, 2017), American University in Cairo, Egypt, Master of Public Administration Program, 2017), ISCTE-Instituto Universitário de Lisboa, Portugal (Master of Science in Public Administration Program, 2017), Ghent University, Belgium (Master of Science in Public Administration and Management Program, 2019).
9   School of Public Affairs and Administration at Rutgers University – Newark, United States (Doctor of Philosophy in Public Administration Program, 2015).
10 School of Public Affairs and Administration at Rutgers University – Newark, United States (Training and Certificate Programs, 2015).

D. ***Decision/Judgement***. Based on the report of the site team and its internal analysis, ICAPA gives its judgment—which may be: accreditation, postpone accreditation, or deny accreditation—and communicates its decision.

ICAPA assess the program using institutional and program mission–related criteria, with the latter subdivided into four subcategories: program development and review, program content, program management, and program performance, each with their own indicators. It measures progress on institutional and program-related criteria on Likert Scale Items: 0=Non-Existent, 1=Basic Level, 4=Intermediate Level, and 7=High Performing (for details see http://www.atlas101.ca/pm/wp-content/uploads/2015/12/UN-IASIA_Standards.pdf). Box 1 presents the eights ICAPA standards and their descriptions. For details and updates see https://iasia.iias-iisa.org/accreditation.php.

Box 1. ICAPA on Standards of Excellence

1. **Public Service Commitment**: The faculty and administration of the program are defined by their fundamental commitment to public service. They are, in all of their activities (teaching, training, research, technical assistance and other service activities), at all times absolutely committed to the advancement of the public interest and the building of democratic institutions. This is true within all facets of the program, including internal organizational arrangements, as well as programmatic activities at local, regional, national, and international levels.

2. **Advocacy of Public Interest Values**: The program's faculty and administration reflect their commitment to the advancement of public service by both their advocacy for, and their efforts to create, a culture of participation, commitment, responsiveness, and accountability in all of those organizations and institutions with which they come into contact. In so doing, both by pedagogy and example, they prepare students and trainees to provide the highest quality of public service.

3. **Combining Scholarship, Practice, and Community Service**: Because public administration is an applied science, the faculty and administration of the program are committed to the integration of theory and practice and, as such, the program draws upon knowledge and understanding generated both by the highest quality of research and the most outstanding practical experience. Consequently, the faculty, administration, and students of the program are actively engaged through its teaching, training, research, and service activities with all of their stake holder communities, from the smallest village or city neighborhood to the global community at large.

4. **The Faculty Are Central**: The commitment and quality of the faculty (and / or trainers) is central to the achievement of program goals in all areas of activity.

Consequently, there must be, especially in degree-granting programs, a full-time, core faculty committed to the highest standards of teaching, training, and research and possessing the authority and responsibility appropriate to accepted standards of faculty program governance. This faculty must be paid at a level that allows them to devote the totality of their professional activities to the achievements of the goals and purposes of the program and must be available in adequate numbers consistent with the mission of the program. In that regard, a ratio of one faculty member per twenty graduate level students and at least four full-time faculty members would represent the typical minimum requirements. Faculty teaching responsibilities should not be greater than two academic courses (or their equivalent in a training institution) at any time in the calendar year in order to allow for necessary involvement in research, training, service, and technical assistance activities.

5. **Inclusiveness Is at the Heart of the Program**: A critical element in the achievement of excellence in public administration education and training is an unwavering commitment on the part of faculty and administration to the diversity of ideas and participation. The people who participate in programs, including students, trainees, trainers, administrators, and faculty, should come from all of the different racial, ethnic, and demographic communities of the society. The ideas, concepts, theories, and practices addressed in the program should represent a broad variety of intellectual interests and approaches. Inclusiveness in terms of individual involvement (including sensitivity to issues of ethnicity, nationality, race, gender orientation, and accessibility to all) within a program also serves to encourage inclusiveness in terms of ideas. Both forms of inclusiveness, intellectual and participatory, are the hallmarks of excellent programs.

6. **A Curriculum That Is Purposeful and Responsive**: A principal goal of public administration education and training is the development of public administrators who will make strong, positive contributions to the public service generally and, in particular, to the organizations they join, or to which they return. This requires public administration education and training programs to have coherent missions that drive program organization and curriculum development. In addition, it is critical that those who educate and train public administrators communicate and work with and, as appropriate, be responsive to the organizations for which they are preparing students and trainees. It also requires that the student and / or trainee be inculcated with a commitment to making a difference and that their education and training prepare them to effectively communicate (both verbally and in writing) with the people that they work with.

7. **Adequate Resources Are Critical**: An important prerequisite to creating a program of excellence in public administration education and training is the

availability of adequate resources. Many different kinds of resources are required, including facilities, technology, library resources, and student services (in terms of assistance with meeting such basic needs as housing, health care, etc.). The availability of these resources is obviously a function of the availability of adequate financial resources. Those financial resources must be able to sustain full-time faculty and / or trainers, provide needed assistance to students and faculty (such as funding to participate in international conferences, etc.), and ensure the availability of adequate classroom, research, training, and meeting space, as well as individual offices for each faculty member and as needed for students.

8. **Balancing Collaboration and Competition**: Finally, and most importantly, there must be among the program faculty, trainers, administrators, and students and / or trainees a sense of common purpose and mission deriving from the program's commitment to the advancing of the public interest. There must also be a sense of determination, indeed, even competitiveness, that drives the program to be the best and creates a desire to meet and exceed world class standards of excellence.

Source: Adopted from Rosenbaum (2015:38-40)

4.4.2. European Association for Public Administration Accreditation (EAPAA)

Founded in 1999, the European Association for Public Administration Accreditation (EAPAA) conducts voluntary accreditation through the Accreditation Committee for public administration programs, in the broader sense, in the Council of Europe (Jabes 2008; Daemen & van der Krogt 2008; Van der Krogt 2015; Brans & Coenen 2016). EAPAA focuses on improving and maintaining the quality of PA programs (Nemec 2008; Klun & Reichard 2019) and has been accrediting PA programs following the Bologna process since the 2000s (Jabes\2008). As of 2019, EAPAA had accredited close to fifty programs in twelve different countries, and many PA programs have started seeking accreditation from it (Klun & Reichard 2019).

Partly due to benchmarking and experience-sharing activities, EAPAA adopted NASPAA's system and uses a mission- and peer-based and standards-based evaluation system (Nemec 2008; Van der Krogt 2015; Rosenbaum 2015; Klun & Reichard 2019). As in NASPAA, EAPAA also started its function by accrediting masters PA programs (Rosenbaum, 2015), but recently it has also begun accrediting bachelor programs (Klun & Reichard 2019). It also follows the same approach as NASPAA: self-evaluation according to the template, site visit, reporting, and judgment by an independent accreditation committee (Nemec 2008; Brans & Coenen 2016). Furthermore, EPAA uses more of a bottom-up approach and evaluates the program against its own mission and target (Pattyn et al. 2008; Brans & Coenen 2016). However, its evaluation standards are not the same as those of NASPAA (Van der Krogt 2015). For details and updates see https://www.eapaa.eu.

EAPAA's entry requirements and general standards are:
- Geography (countries of the Council of Europe) (entry requirement)
- Program longevity (at least two cohorts of graduates) (entry requirement)
- Mission-based curriculum content
- Quality improvement and assurance
- Innovation
- Student assessment
- Program jurisdiction
- Faculty nucleus and qualifications
- Student admission
- Support services and facilities
- Student services
- Public relations

4.4.3. African Higher Education Quality Assurance and Accreditation (AHEQAA)

Based on the Bologna approach that seeks to ensure the harmonization of education in Europe and in line with its Agenda 2063—the Africa We Want—the African Union, in the framework of Africa-EU Strategic Partnership, has also called for harmonization and strengthening the quality of HEIs and ensuring intra-Africa academic mobility (AU, 2014b). The initiative was facilitated by the African Union Commission (AUC) in partnership with the European Union (and EU institutions, and the Association of African Universities.

The project initiated the Harmonization of African Higher Education Quality Assurance and Accreditation (HAQAA) and the Pan-African Quality Assurance and Accreditation Framework (PAQAF). It was argued that harmonized criteria and standards not only enhance a shared view on the quality and standards but also provide frameworks for comparable quality assessment. HAQAA was implemented by the Association of African Universities, the German Academic Exchange Service (DAAD), the European University Association (EUA), the European Association for Quality Assurance in Higher Education (ENQA), and the University of Barcelona (the coordinator).

PAQAF is developed based on national and regional qualification frameworks and seeks to facilitate collaboration and networking between quality assurance and accreditation agencies.

To implement PAQAF, the project developed the African Standards and Guidelines for Quality Assurance in Higher Education (ASG-QA) and the African Quality Rating Mechanism (AQRM) and created the African Quality Assurance Network (AFRIQAN)[11]. AFRIQAN focuses on harmonizing qualifications and improving quality in higher education (AU 2014b). ASG-QA sets out standards and guidelines for internal quality assurance, external quality assurance, and internal quality assurance for quality assurance agencies (HAQAA Consortium 2018a). AHEQAA focuses on institutional rating but has not established an accreditation commission yet. As a result, currently, it focuses only on evaluating and rating African HEIs and providing feedback.

The standards for internal quality assurance are:
1. Vision, mission and strategic objectives
2. Governance and management
3. Human resources
4. Financial resource management
5. Infrastructure and facilities
6. Student recruitment, admission, certification, and support services
7. Design, approval, monitoring, and evaluation of study programs
8. Teaching, learning, and assessment
9. Research and innovation
10. Community engagement
11. Information management system
12. Public communication
13. Collaboration, staff and student mobility

The standards for external quality assurance are as follows.
1. Objectives of external quality assurance and consideration for internal quality assurance
2. Designing external quality assurance mechanisms fit for purpose
3. Implementation processes of external quality assurance
4. Independence of evaluation
5. Decision and reporting of external quality assurance outcomes
6. Periodic review of institutions and programs
7. Complaints and appeals

11   Is flagship programme of the AAU

The standards for internal quality assurance for quality assurance agencies are:
1. Legal status
2. Vision and mission statement
3. Governance and management
4. Independence of QAA
5. Policies, processes, and activities
6. Internal quality assurance
7. Financial and human resources
8. Benchmarking, networking, and collaboration
9. Periodic review of QAAs

AQRM is an HEI quality assessment tool in Africa and aims to support continuous quality improvement. It was adopted in 2017 and uses internal (self-rating) and external (peer rating) mechanisms to assess the quality of HEIs (not of programs), and rates them on a 0–4 scale (0=poor quality, 4=excellent quality) on both an institutional level and program level. AQRM has six institutional-level and five program-level criteria, both respectively comprising forty-nine and thirty-five standards (HAQAA Consortium 2018b). These are as follows:

A. Institutional Level Criteria.
   1. Governance and management (9 standards),
   2. Infrastructure (8 standards),
   3. Finances (6 standards),
   4. Teaching and learning (9 standards),
   5. Research, publication, and innovation (10), and
   6. Community / societal engagement (7 standards).

B. Program Level Criteria
   1. Program planning and management (8 standards),
   2. Curriculum development (7 standards),
   3. Teaching and learning (6 standards),
   4. Assessment (6 standards),
   5. Program results (8 standards)

In 2018 fifteen African universities volunteered and to be rated using AQRM criteria (HAQAA Consortium, 2018b). The African Union Commission (AUC) also developed a ten-year continental education strategy (2016–2025) that is rooted in African core values and Agenda 2063, consisting of twelve strategic objectives (AU 2016). Five of the strategic objectives (SO) that are directly related to higher education are SO1 (Revitalize the teaching profession to ensure quality and relevance of education); SO9 (Revitalize and expand tertiary education, research, and innovation); SO10 (Promote peace education and conflict management), SO11 (Improve management of education system and build capacity for data management and use), and SO12 (collaborate with stakeholders). PA programs can use AQRM standards and criteria for self-rating (internal evaluation).

4.4.4. National Association of Schools of Public Affairs and Administration (NASPAA)

The National Association of Schools of Public Affairs and Administration (NASPAA) was founded in 1970, in the United States. It changed its name to Network of Schools of Public Policy, Affairs, and Administration in 2013 but retained its well-known acronym (McFarland 2015; van der Krogt 2015). NASPAA is committed to promoting excellence in education and training for public service by developing and using standards in public administration education and training in the United States (Mishra 2015). It began operations by rostering master's programs in public administration (van der Krogt 2015, 99), and as of 1982, out of ninety-two programs that submitted their self-study reports, seventy-three had undergone site visits, and sixty-two were rostered (Daniels & Johansen 1985). NASPAA began formal accreditation in 1983 (Guy & Stillman 2016).

In 2009 NASPAA decided to move beyond the United States. However, NASPAA is only interested in evaluating and accrediting overseas programs that sufficiently demonstrate "American-style" features (McFarland 2015). Holmes (2020) finds that NASPAA accredited PA programs in seven countries (USA, Colombia, China, Egypt, New Zealand, South Korea, Venezuela).

During the early years, NASPAA applied a highly structured standard but moved to a mission-based process in the early 1990s (McFarland 2015; Holmes 2020). Driven by the voluntary peer review system, NASPAA accredits PA programs through the Commission on Peer Review and Accreditation for seven years (van der Krogt 2015). In recent years, NASPAA standards have also given due attention to "public values and student competencies" (van der Krogt 2015, 110). These include advancing public interest with accountability and transparency; professional competencies, efficiency, and objectivity in public services; acting ethically to ensure public trust; and demonstrating respect, equity, and fairness in public services, which distinguishes PA graduates from other program graduates (Holmes 2020).

Van der Krogt (2015) notes that NASPAA continuously revise its standards. The seven NASPAA standards, as of 2015, are as follows:
1. Managing the program strategically
2. Matching governance with the mission
3. Matching operations with the mission: Faculty performance
4. Matching operations with the mission: Serving students
5. Matching operations with the mission: Student learning
6. Matching resources with the mission
7. Matching communications with the mission

Van der Krogt (2015) and McFarland (2015) identify three stages in the NASPAA accreditation process, which are almost similar to ICAPA's, suggesting ICAPA adopted the accreditation process from NASPAA. The first stage concerns self-evaluation report preparation and submission and review by the Commission. Next, the Commission establishes a site visit team to evaluate the program and reports its finding to the Commission.

The NASPAA site visit team is composed of two academics and one practitioner. The team is responsible for verifying and clarifying self-study reports, collecting relevant information, and sharing experience and innovative—ideas among peers (Holmes, 2020). Finally, the Commission—based on the findings of the team and its analysis—either accredits, delays accreditation, or denies accreditation. Details and updates can be found at https://www.naspaa.org.

4.4.5. Other National Experiences: Africa

In Africa, higher education quality assurance goes back to the founding of the first universities, where the qualities of African universities were assured by European universities and / or the colonial education system (Crossman 1999; Hayward 2006; Tamrat 2020). After political independence, following the unprecedented student enrollment in African higher education and the rapid growth of private higher education institutions, since the late 1980s, and reacting to the inability of external examiners to provide quality assurance services and due to increasing concerns about the quality of education and other factors, many African countries established national quality assurance and accreditation agencies (Hayward 2006; HAQAA Consortium 2018c). Several African states have developed criteria and standards for internal and external quality ratings (Hayward, 2006).

Kenya (1985), Nigeria (1990–1991), and Cameroon (1991) are among the first African countries that established an accreditation agency responsible for assuring and accrediting the quality and relevance of higher education institutions and their programs. Cameroon was also the first country to initiate the accreditation of private universities in 1991 (Hayward 2006). Table 3 presents a list of national higher education quality assurance institutions in thirty-six African countries.

Overall, many African countries have increasing concerns and are pushing to improve and assure the quality of higher education and their programs. However, none of the national higher education quality assurance institutions have adequate capacity and very little is known about their practice (Hayward 2006), suggesting Africa tends to lag behind the world in creating a knowledge society.

Table 3. Names of Higher Education Quality Assurance and Accreditation Agencies in 36 African Countries from 2016 to 2017

Country	Name of Quality Agency
Algeria	National Commission for Quality Assurance Implementation in Higher Education (CIAQES)
Angola	National Institute for the Assessment and Accreditation of Higher Education (INAAES)
Benin	Ministry of Higher Education and Scientific Research
Botswana	Botswana Qualifications Authority (BQA)
Burkina Faso	African and Malagasy Council for Higher Education (CAMES)
Burundi	National Commission for Higher Education (NCHE)
Cameron	National Commission on Private Higher Education (NCPHE)
CAR	National Agency for Quality Assurance and Accreditation of Higher Education
DRC	National Quality Assurance Agency
Egypt	National Authority for Quality Assurance and Accreditation of Education (NAQAAE)
Ethiopia	Higher Education Relevance and Quality Agency (HERQA) since 2021 called Education and Training Authority (ETA)
Gambia	National Accreditation and Quality Assurance Authority (NAQAA)
Ghana	National Accreditation Board (NAB)
Kenya	Commission for Higher Education (CUE)
Lesotho	Commission for Higher Education (CHE)
Liberia	National Commission on Higher Education (NCHE)

Country	Name of Quality Agency
Libya	The Executive Committee for Quality Assurance in Higher Education (ECQAHE)
Madagascar	Accreditation and Quality Assurance Agency
Malawi	Malawi Bureau of Standards (MBS)
Mali	National Directorate of Higher Education and Scientific Research (DNESRS)
Mauritius	Tertiary Education Commission (TEC)
Morocco	National Agency for Evaluation and Quality Assurance for Higher Education (NAEQAHE)
Mozambique	National Council for Accreditation and Quality Assurance in Higher Education (CNAQ)
Namibia	National Council for Higher Education (NCHE)
Nigeria	National Universities Commission (NUC)
Rwanda	Higher Education Council
Senegal	National Authority for Quality Assurance in Higher Education, Research and Innovation
Seychelles	Seychelles Qualifications Authority (SQA)
South Africa	Council on Higher Education (CHE)
Sudan	Evaluation and Accreditation Corporation (EVAC)
Tanzania	Higher Education Accreditation Council (HEAC)
Togo	Ministry of Higher Education and Scientific Research
Tunisia	National Authority for Evaluation, Quality Assurance and Accreditation (IEAQA)
Uganda	National Council for Higher Education (NCHE)
Zambia	Higher Education Authority (HEA)
Zimbabwe	Zimbabwe Council for Higher Education (ZIMCHE)

Source: Compiled from HAQAA Consortium (2018C)

Ethiopian Higher Education Relevance and Quality Agency (HERQA)/ Education and Training Authority (ETA)

Cognizant of the quality and relevance challenges, Ethiopia established the Higher Education Relevance and Quality Agency (HERQA) in 2003 (Tamrat 2020). HERQA is responsible for evaluating and assuring the quality and relevance of all HEIs and their programs, which in 2018 amounted to fifty public universities and 250 private higher education institutions (Tamrat

2020). However, due to its inadequate institutional capacity, HERQA has been focusing on accrediting private HEIs and their programs.[12]

Indeed, in Ethiopia public HEIs are not subjected to accreditation by HERQA but are governed by parliamentary acts (Adamu & Addamu 2012). The parliamentary proclamations set out that the universities are responsible for establishing internal quality assurance systems, developing quality standards, and ensuring the quality and relevance of their programs (FDRE 2009, 2019). The internal quality assurance system of public universities, however, has weaknesses that include lack of sufficient integration of the quality assurance unit with the university system, inadequate autonomy of the quality assurance unit, insufficient university support for its activities, and insufficient stakeholder participation (Tamrat 2020).

HERQA was accountable to the Ministry of Higher Education (MoE) from 2003 to 2018, then to the Ministry of Science and Higher Education (Moshe) from 2019 to 2021. HERQA changed its name into Education and Training Authority (ETA), in 2021 and accountable to MoE (2021–). HERQA provided institutional accreditation (for private HEIs) and conduct institutional quality audits (both for private and public HEIs). HERQA's role in public higher education primarily focused on providing training and advice. Recently, public HEIs started internally using HERQA standards to evaluate the relevance and quality of their education programs. ETA has started program-level accreditation for health-related disciplines for Public HEIs. The efforts of the ETA to accredit PA programs are to be seen. ETA has not changed HERQA's focus areas and steps in institutional audit.

The following are ten focus areas of HERQ/ETA
- Vision, mission, and educational goals;
- Governance and management system;
- Infrastructure and learning resources;
- Academic and support staff;
- Student admission and support services;
- Program relevance and curriculum;
- Teaching, learning, and assessment;
- Student progression and graduate outcomes;
- Research and outreach activities; and
- Internal quality assurance

---

12 HERQA accredits private HEIs for three years.

HERQA/ETA applies eight major steps in an institutional audit:
1. HEI carries out self-evaluation
2. HEI and HERQA/ ETA agree on a date for institutional quality audit
3. HERQA/ ETA establishes external quality audit team in consultation with HEI
4. HERQA/ ETA's preliminary briefing visit to HEI
5. HERQA's external auditors make audit visit to HEI
6. HERQA/ ETA issues a quality audit report
7. HEI prepares action plan to enhance quality
8. HERQA/ ETA revisits HEIs to follow up

4.5. The Debate on Public Administration Program Accreditation

There are three equally important debates on accreditation. The first concerns the types of accreditation. As Haug (2003) put it, the question is, should an organization seek institutional or program accreditation or both at the same time? Is program accreditation affordable for the HEI in question? While quality assurance and accreditation agencies such as African quality assurance and accreditation agencies and HERQA accredit institutions, organizations such as ICAPA, EAPPA, and NASPAA offer accreditation for the PA program. For Haug (2003), in the future, organizations are more likely to focus on institutional accreditation complementing program accreditation in some fields that could vary between systems, institutions, and specialization and program levels.

Within this debate, there is a sub-debate on program accreditation. For example, one of the key questions concerns the scope of PA program accreditation. EAPAA accredits public administration programs in the broader sense (Van der Krogt 2015; Brans & Coenen 2016), but can Tourism Management and Public Finance, for instance, be accredited by EAPAA? Likewise, NASPAA accredits programs, such as public administration, public policy, and public affairs (Guy & Stillman 2016). However, the disciplinary boundaries (scope) and nomenclatures of the program within NASPAA's mandate are unclear (Breaux et al. 2003). This also holds for ICAPA. For example, can ICAPA accredit Public Financial Management, and Governance and Development? There is no "one-size-fits-all" answer for this. The accrediting bodies usually decide which programs (nomenclature) can be accredited. One of the criteria for decision is courses included in the curriculum. For example, although NASPAA respects curriculum and / or mission diversity, it "requires a public administration or public affairs core curriculum to expose students to the environmental context in which public administration occurs and professional administrator interaction with the environment (administrative responsiveness). Core curriculum content also must cover the managerial and analytical skills that public administrators use (professional administration)" (Breaux et al. 2003, 260).

The second area of debate is on three principles of accreditation, namely market, network (peers), and hierarchy. The market principle is akin to NPM and emphasizes that the market is the organizing principle of accreditation. An example is MBA program accreditation. Peer (network) accreditation focuses on learning rather than on profit maximization. ICAPA, EAPPA, and NASPAA are examples of peer-based PA program accreditation institutions. The hierarchy advocate for top-down approaches and focuses on controlling and vertical coordination. Many governmental national quality assurance and accreditation institutions fall into this category.

The third debatable issue is who is eligible for accreditation. One of the debates is who has the legitimacy to accredit PA programs designed to produce profession-oriented civil servants and offered by national / federal or regional schools or universities of civil service. Are they academicians or practitioners? The other area of debate here is who is eligible for membership in PA program accrediting bodies (committees or commissions): (a) academics, (b) practitioners, (c) students, (d) employers, (e) state / government representatives, or who else? What is the composition of the committee? Experiences vary from country to country, and hence there is no single way of doing it. This issue could be influenced by the accreditation approach / philosophy followed by a given accrediting network / association / institution. For example, if the accreditation approach followed is peer-oriented and if the subjects of accreditation are academic-oriented PAs, the accrediting body could be dominated by academia. The composition of the accreditation commission could differ if the accreditation approach pursued is market-oriented, peer, or formal / state-based. Finally, there is also debate and / or a difference in practice on the level of PA programs that need accreditation (BA, master's, and PhD or non-degree levels). Thus, again, the level of program accreditation varies from country to country and from institution to institution.

For other Western debates on accreditation, you can consult: https://eclass.upatras.gr/modules/document/file.php/PN1589/Accreditation%20and%20Evaluation%20in%20the%20EHEA.pdf#page=54.

4.6. The Costs and Challenges of Accreditation

Notwithstanding the benefits, accreditation also involves costs and challenges. Some of them could be significantly reduced. The major costs and challenges are discussed below:

Monetary costs

The cost of accreditation is a critical factor and tends to be a critical issue. Accreditation takes money and staff resources (Hayward 2006; Holmes 2020). For example, while NASPAA charges over $5000 dollars in accreditation fees (Holmes 2020), ICAPA requires a EU 4000 accreditation fee paid to IASIA (Rosenbaum 2015). The reaccreditation fee of both NASPAA and ICAPA is also high. Furthermore, the accreditation-seeking organizations or programs also needs to cover travel and accommodation costs, as well as other related expenses of the site visit team and hosting groups and to compensate faculty or staff time for their participation in the accreditation process (Holmes 2020). The cost of accreditation could be much higher. Unlike in the USA and Europe, where the site visiting peers are not paid for their services, in other countries, such as in Africa, peer reviewers and others involved in the site visit seek payment (Hayward 2006), suggesting monetary cost could be a serious challenge, particularly for financially weak HEIs. Nevertheless, such HEIs can partner with national quality assurance agencies, professional associations, seeking funding and mobilizing resources from other sources (Hayward 2006).

Bureaucratic costs

Although no one is against quality improvement, some people criticize the process and question who should participate in the accreditation, arguing that accreditation is not only time-consuming but also allows the accrediting agency to impose its will on the institutions or programs. They also argue that such imposition contradicts with professional values (Hayward 2006; Pham 2018). This critic reminds us of the need to minimize bureaucratic hurdles. To do so, effective time management, promoting evidence-based stakeholder dialogue, and ensuring transparency and accountability in the accreditation process would be useful.

Quality and objectivity of assessment

Some people argue that the link between accreditation and quality improvement in teaching-learning is weak, while others question the quality and objectivity of assessment (Pham 2018). Nevertheless, effective collaboration between the site visit team, the faculty, and other stakeholders would be helpful to address this challenge. One way to do this is to rely on multiple data sources, consultation, and participants' reflections. Establishing an independent site visit team composed of academics (peers) and practitioners is also crucial.

Inadequate human capacity
The availability of qualified human resources is one of the critical issues in accreditation, particularly the availability of qualified faculty staff. The quality of peer reviewers also matters. Qualified peer reviewers ensure the quality of the assessment and the legitimacy of the accreditation process. However, it could be challenging to get competent professionals who can serve as peer reviewers (Hayward 2006). The challenge increases when the senior professionals hold multiple responsibilities such as administration, teaching, research, consultancy, and committee work, which could be more challenging in Africa (Hayward 2006). Working with professional associations and international accreditation agencies might reduce this challenge.

4.7. Conclusions

Accreditation has both benefits and costs. There are different overlapping dimensions and types of evaluation. PA program evaluators can choose between varied dimensions and types of evaluations. PA program accreditation evaluation, however, entails external, formative, voluntary, peer, and mission-based evaluation at BA, MA, and PhD levels, and sometimes at the non-degree program level as well. There are three major conclusions to be drawn from the discussion in this chapter.

First, in recent years, much attention has been given to ensuring the quality and the relevance of PA education and training through international (ICAPA), regional / continental (EAPAA), and national (e.g., NASPAA) quality assurance and accreditation agencies. The processes of quality assurance and accreditation followed by institution / agencies are similar: self-assessment, site visit, reporting, and decision / judgment.

Second, in the framework of the Africa-EU Strategic Partnership, Africa has adopted the Bologna process to harmonize educational curricula and strengthen the quality of higher education institutions and ensure intra-Africa academic mobility. To this end, the continent, among other things, has recently introduced the Pan-African Quality Assurance and Accreditation Framework, the African Standards and Guidelines for Quality Assurance in

Higher Education, and the African Quality Rating Mechanism and created the African Quality Assurance Network. Institutional rating started in 2018. Finally, several African governments have established national quality assurance and accreditation agencies. Yet, these agencies, including the Ethiopian HERQA/ ETA, have inadequate institutional capacity.

Chapter Five
Steps to Ethiopian Public Administration Program Accreditation

5.1. Beyond De Jure Accreditation

Many public universities in several countries are accredited by parliamentary acts, suggesting they are not accredited by an independent agency as result of an accreditation process (Hayward 2006; Adamu & Addamu 2012). This holds true in many countries, particularly in Africa and other developing countries, including Ethiopia. Such HEIs have de jure accreditation status (Hayward 2006). This practice could jeopardize the quality and relevance of education and the accountability of HEIs, although universities that have internal quality assurance mechanisms can reduce the challenges and problems arising from this situation.

5.2. How to Start and Conduct Accreditation?

Already much has been said about the accreditation process. Yet, the institutions and program managers need to understand value of accreditation, the accreditation process, and how to start and conduct the accreditation (Holmes 2020). This involves a set of interrelated activities, which have already been mentioned above but are repeated here for emphasis and elaborations.

At the outset, the accreditation-seeking institution or program needs to recognize the values of accreditation (including program improvement, internal and external recognition, and support of stakeholders) and the time and resources that are to be dedicated to accreditation (Holmes 2020).

Second, the institution or program needs to distinguish the requirements to initiate the accreditation. Some of the requirements could depend on whether the institution is private or public, and on the number of years the program is in operation. For the latter, a defined minimum number of years the program is in operation is the necessity. To operate, private HEIs ideally need to be accredited, at least, for some programs. For public HEIs, de jure accreditation is often the reality. However, a minimum number of years in operation could be comparable for private and public institutions, say, for example, the program needs to have at least two graduating cohorts. As such, the requirements could vary between accreditation agencies. For example, to be eligible for NASPAA accreditation, the program must be: (1) officially recognized nationally, regionally, or internationally; (2) the mission, governance, and curriculum of the program must emphasize public values; (3) the program must be dedicated to preparing students to be leaders, managers, and analysts in public administration and public policy professions; and (4) the normal study semester and / or hour expectations should be sufficient (Holmes 2020).

Once the attainment of the preliminary requirements is confirmed, the next step is developing a self-assessment report and institutional application to enter into the peer-review process. The self-assessment report is better written by a team comprising relevant professionals and backed by an inclusive internal stakeholders' review. The internal review would be helpful to improve the quality and integrate the insights of stakeholders in the report.

Third, the self-assessment report needs to be submitted to the accreditation agency in time. This allows the agency to review the self-assessment report and establish the relevant and representative site visit team (peers). The report enables the accreditation agency to identify additional clarifications and information before the site visit and the agency's decision to conduct site visit (Holmes 2020).

The final step is creating a conducive environment for the site visit team. This requires consultation to set the time for the visit and evaluation. Ideally, the team should have adequate time for the field visit; two to five days according to ICAPA and 2.5 days according to NASPAA. The site visit team is expected to uphold professional integrity in its evaluation and present a comprehensive report comprising recommendations based on which the accreditation agency passes its final judgments and communicates the decision to the requesting institution.

5.3. PA Program Accreditation Initiative in Ethiopia: Lessons from AAU and AU

> **Addis Ababa University (AAU): Institutional Background**
>
> AAU was founded as the University College of Addis Ababa (UCAA) in 1950, named Haile Selassie I University (HSIU) in 1961, and became Addis Ababa University in 1974. Beginning with 33 students in 1950, AAU in the 2020 / 21 Academic Year enrolled over 47,610 students (29,872 undergraduate, 15,398 master's, and 2,340

PhD students) and counts 8,709 staff (3,110 academics, 4,346 administrative support staff, and 1,253 health professionals). Currently, the university comprises fourteen campuses, ten colleges, two technology institutes, and four institutes, all organized into fifty-five departments, thirteen centers, nineteen schools, and two teaching hospitals. The University runs 76 undergraduate and 385 graduate programs and offers various specializations in health sciences. The university is heading toward becoming a graduate research university. Since its establishment, over 228,000 students have graduated from AAU. According to the Times Higher Education World University Rankings 2022, Addis Ababa University is 1st in East Africa, 6th in Africa, and 402nd in the world.

The mission of Addis Ababa University, as a research university, is to produce competent graduates, pursue problem-solving and knowledge-expanding research outputs, and actively participate in scholarly community engagements to contribute to national, continental, and global development. The vision of AAU is to: "Become a world class university and the leading research university in East Africa"

AAU is the pioneer for PA education in Ethiopia. It launched a BA in the 1950s, an MA in 2005, and a PhD in 2010. Presently, the Department of Public Administration and Development Management has twenty-one academic staff, of which fourteen have MA degrees (12 male and 2 female) and seven have PhDs (6 male and 1 female). It currently enrolls 273 BA (134 Male and 139 female), 53 MA (40 male and 13 female) and 14 PhD (13 male and 1 female) students.

Ambo University (AU): Institutional Background

Founded in 1946 as the Ambo School of Agriculture, AU is the first agricultural HEI in Ethiopia. The university has experienced various levels of institutional development. In 1958 it became Ambo Agriculture and Forestry Secondary School, was renamed Ambo Institute of Agriculture in 1967, and became Ambo Junior College of Agriculture in 1974. In 1992 it shed the "junior" status in and became the Ambo College of Agriculture. In 2003 it was affiliated with Jimma University, renamed Jimma University-Ambo College, and began offering undergraduate degree programs. In 2008 it became the autonomous Ambo University College and became Ambo University in 2009. Presently, AU has eight colleges / institutes / schools and one teaching hospital situated on four campuses: Main Campus, Institute of Technology (Artist Hachalu Hundesa Campus), Guder Mamo Mezemir Campus (Agriculture), and Woliso Campus and runs 71 undergraduate, 75 master's, 10 PhD, and four specialty programs. Currently, AU has over 21,000 students and 1,606 academic staff (1,365 male and 241 female), of which 415 were first degree, 999 master's, 164 PhDs, and 28 specialists. It has the vision of becoming, by 2030, one of the most prestigious universities in East Africa, excelling in academics, research, and community service, giving its utmost attention to quality education.

AU began offering a BA in Development Management in 2006, which transformed into the BA in Public Administration and Development Management in the 2011 / 2012 Academic Year. It began offering an MA in Development Management in 2016. Currently, the Department of Public Administration and Development Management on the Main Campus has 9 male academic staff, of whom 8 hold an MA and 1 has a PhD. The department has enrolled 45 BA (28 Male and 17 Female) and 102 MA (76 male and 26 female) students. The department at Woliso Campus has five male (3 hold an MA and 2 have a BA) and 3 female (1 has an MA and 2 hold a BA) academic staff. The department has enrolled 41 BA students of which 21 were male and 20 were female. The departments at both the Main and Woliso Campuses uses similar nationally harmonized BA curriculum.

The AAU and AU PA Education Program Accreditation Initiative
In Ethiopia, the need to ensure the quality and relevance of higher education has gotten increasing attention following the massive expansion of HEIs since the 2000s. The quality and relevance of education have become the priority for the government (MoFED 2010; MoE 2010; MoE 2015; NPC 2016), which established HERQA in 2003. Improving and assuring the relevance of PA education and training programs is also a critical issue among Ethiopian PA scholars. Stakeholders discussed these issues at the AU and KU Leuven participatory workshop (August 27, 2012), at the first National PA Conference organized by Ambo University and KU Leuven in collaboration with CCRDA, funded by VLIR-UOS (September 21, 2015), both events contributing to the founding of EPAA on September 29, 2016 (AAU) and launched at Addis Ababa University (February 8, 2018) (Debela et al. 2020).

A concrete action toward accrediting PA education at Ambo University and Addis Ababa University took place in 2017. Drawing on the momentum and the interest since 2012, in 2017, AU, KU Leuven, and AAU developed the project "Professionalizing Ethiopian Public Administration to Support Development Practitioners" and funded by VLIR-UOS.

One of the results foreseen in the framework of the project was that AU and AAU, respectively, should undergo an international accreditation process and receive accreditation for their BA and MA programs. To this end, AU and AAU have self-evaluated their PA programs using ICAPA's standards. Meanwhile, AAU also wanted to accredit its BA PA program. At two virtual workshops organized by Public Governance Institute (KU Leuven), the project partners and other participants discussed the draft self-assessment reports of the two universities. The reflection and feedback enabled AU and AAU to enrich the self-assessment reports. In addition, the AU and AAU PA program accreditation team visited the Public Governance Institute (KU Leuven). At the meeting, the participants discussed PA program accreditation in general, the accreditation experience of the Public Governance Institute, and the

AU and AAU self-assessment report. The self-evaluation process and the virtual and face-to-face meetings allowed AU and AAU to update the self-assessment reports and submit them to ICAPA. ICAPA will conduct the site visit in September 2022 and no later than the end of 2022.

The lessons from the self-evaluation (assessment) report
The following are the key lessons from the AU and AAU experiences:
Lesson 1: The ICAPA standards are complementary to HERQA standards.
Lesson 2: The relevance of seeking an international PA program accreditation.
Lesson 3: The necessity to continuously conduct internal self-assessment using reliable standards to improve and maintain the quality and relevance of PA education and training programs.
Lesson 4: The need for critical reflection and dialogue with PA education and training program stakeholders.
Lesson 5: The necessity for strengthening institutional and PA staff commitment to engage in the self-assessment process and improve the quality and relevance of the PA program.
Lesson 6: The necessity of effective data management, documentation, and a quality self-assessment report.
Lesson 7: The importance of peer learning to improve the quality and relevance of the PA program and ensure the quality of the self-assessment report.

5.4. How to Organize the Accreditation

The literature identifies the following important recommendations for an effective accreditation process, which are also relevant for Ethiopian PA education and training programs:

Making the assessment process meaningful. To overcome the challenges in the accreditation process, it is crucial to ensure it is mission-driven and based on defined Program goals and students' learning outcomes. A clear mission and related learning outcomes are the keys to quality and meaningful assessment (Holmes 2020).

Engage faculty early and often. The faculty and the department that determines the governance and implementation of the program not only play a critical role in the accreditation process but also sustain program quality and relevance (Holmes 2020). Faculty members need to also engage in accreditation data collection, self-assessment reports, and site visits. To enhance their engagement, as Holmes (2020) suggests, it is crucial to (1) assign and compensate faculty members to coordinate the accreditation process; (2) organize faculty meetings to discuss and reflect on the program and self-study report, and (3) facilitate sharing, listening, and reporting among faculty members.

Leverage significant stakeholders. The accreditation process should be inclusive of internal and external stakeholders. The participation of the internal stakeholder (faculty, students, and university officials) and external stakeholders (such as alumni, prospective employers, university partners, relevant government institutions) in the accreditation process highlights valuable perspectives and ensures sustained support in the accreditation process and beyond (Holmes 2020).

Compose the self-assessment (study) report. A self-study (assessment) report is the most critical component in the accreditation process. The self-assessment needs to be comprehensive, based on evidence, and follow the template. It also needs to demonstrate the connection between program mission, program goals, faculty and student support, institutional resources, and the implementation of universal competencies (Holmes 2020). It should also clarify the purpose, focus, contexts, and the realities and expectations to concerned parties and the site visit team (Lubinescu et al. 2001).

Embrace the site visit: How to organize it? A site visit is a rewarding component of the accreditation process. The site visit allows peers to share experiences and lessons among the public administration community (academic and practitioner). At the end of the site visit, the team needs to report and reflect on the observations about the program to core faculty members (Holmes 2020).

It would be difficult for peers to be objective enough in their evaluation (van der Krogt 2015). To address the challenge, van der Krogt (2015) suggests the site visit team should be composed of, among others, peers from another country and representatives of practitioners, students, and / or alumni. For example, while NASPAA's site visit team consists of program faculty, students, alumni, the advisory board, university officials, two academics, and one practitioner, ICAPA's site visit team is composed of three members of the ICAPA and one local expert practitioner.

The site visit team needs to hold individual meetings with senior administrators of the program (college / school dean), PA department head, university higher authorities (such as the President), senior and junior faculty, university / college / faculty / school education quality assurance and audit director /

team leader or its equivalent, academic program director or the equivalent, representative groups of students, alumni, program graduates' employing organizations, and relevant community stakeholders that directly benefit from the program. The visiting team is responsible for producing the site visit report and reflection.

Use the available resources. The accreditation institutions provide assistance and guidance throughout the accreditation process (Holmes 2020). For example, IIAS-IASIA / ICAPA organized an open webinar on accreditation in 2022. The speakers at the virtual workshop have had unprecedented experiences in the accreditation process. The website of the accreditation institutions (national and international) also provides helpful information.

5.5. How to Respond to Recommendations and Use Accreditation as Part of Quality Improvement Strategy?

The institution or the program needs to diligently respond to the report, provide detailed and accurate supplementary information and evidence, clearly point out the reservations in the findings of the report and in the decisions of the accreditation agency (Lubinescu et al.,2001).

Even when accreditation is denied, as in the West, the institution or the program is expected to be open to receiving criticism, and the accreditation agency usually makes recommendations for program improvement for the upcoming accreditation period (Lubinescu et al. 2001). The critics may suggest that the institution or program needs to re-evaluate the self-assessment report and accreditation process, develop and monitor improvement plans, monitor improvement activities, and monitor the effects of the improvement to maintain the quality (van der Krogt 2015). Sometimes, an adjustment in some critical features of the program could suffice when total compliance is impossible (Salto 2018).

It should be emphasized that the self-assessment reports, the site visit, the advice, and the rostering by accreditation institutions are of considerable merit in improving the quality and relevance of the PA program (Daniels & Johansen 1985).

5.6. The Need for Capacity Building to Improve and Sustain PA Program Quality

The costs challenges of accreditation discussed in section 4.5 suggest the need to invest in capacity building to improve and sustain the quality and relevance of the PA program. Capacity building is particularly crucial in Ethiopia (Africa) because Ethiopian (African) higher education institutions and accreditation and quality assurance agencies have inadequate institutional and human resource capacity (Hayward 2006). In addition, their internal quality assurance systems are weak when it comes to improving and maintaining the quality and relevance of the educational programs, including the PA program (Hayward 2006; Tamrat 2020).

Interestingly, the weaknesses identified through the accreditation process and the improvement recommendations by the accreditation agency allow organizations to develop relevant capacity-building programs. Self-assessment reports and reflection among faculty members enable the program to identify the capacity gaps. The capacity building could comprise investment in human resources development programs, structural and institutional reforms, and infrastructure.

The human resources capacity-building programs for accreditation need to include national accreditation and quality assurance agency staff, professional accreditors, program managers and faculty members, senior university staff and quality assurance units, peer reviewers, and other relevant stakeholders (Hayward 2006).

5.7. The Need to Establish an Accreditation Unit and a Network of Ethiopian PA Departments within the Ethiopian Public Administration Association (EPAA): The Proposal

The quality and relevance of PA programs can be improved by establishing a National Association of PA departments and a PA accreditation unit. Just like Central and Eastern European countries, Ethiopian PA universities can network with schools and institutes of public administration in African PA universities. The National Association of PA departments, the African Regional and Continental networks of Schools, and the Institutes of Public Administration could not only strengthen the institutional capacity of PA programs but could also be instrumental in the harmonization of African PA programs and the implementation of the Pan-African Quality Assurance and Accreditation Framework. One can draw lessons from the US Network of Schools of Public Policy, Affairs, and Administration and the Network of Asia Pacific Schools and Institutes of Public Administration and Governance (NAPSIPAG) (Jabes 2008). The Network of Schools and Institutes of Public Administration in Central and Eastern Europe (NISPAcee) could also be a good benchmark.

NISPAcee was established in 1994, following the fall of the Soviet Union to strengthen PA teaching and research in the former communist countries (Randma-Liiv et al. 2019), share experiences, and integrate Western PA theories and practices (Jabes 2008). To this end, among others, NISPAcee collaborates with the European Group for Public Administration (EGPA), which is dedicated to the development of public administration from the European perspective (Ongaro 2019). Both EGPA and NISPAcee work with EAPAA (Bouckaert et al. 2019; Randma-Liiv et al. 2019). NISPAcee also works with the European Public Administration Network (EPAN), which is committed to promoting Europeanisation in public administration education (Jabes, 2008).

According to Jabes (2008), a network that promotes PA is useful in enhancing national capacity to promote good governance, strengthen the institutional capacity of member institutions, improve the engagement and professional competence of members, develop professional identity and community, promote and strengthen professional standards and ethics, promote good governance in teaching and research, promote PA discipline and public administration education, promote PA program accreditation, and promote academic freedom (for details, see Jabes 2008).

In Ethiopia, a National Association of PA departments and a PA Accreditation Unit could be established within the Ethiopian Public Administration Association (EPAA). The harmonized PA curriculum would facilitate the accreditation process. The seven EPAA study groups, including the Teaching Public Administration study group, would contribute to the development of PA theories and practice in Ethiopia. Among other things, EPAA is working with Ethiopian public PA universities, the International Institute of Administrative Sciences (IIAS), the African Association of Public Administration and Management (AAPAM), and the Ethiopian Federal House of People Representatives Parliamentary Research Network. Such partnership and network have to be strengthened and sustained, which depends on the commitment of the EPAA Executive Committee, EPAA individual and institutional members (universities hosting PA programs), partners, and other stakeholders.

5.8. Conclusions

The chapter finds interesting results that lead to the following three major conclusions. First, the costs of accreditation cannot sufficiently justify the claim for de jure accreditation, which is the case for many universities in Africa and other developing countries and even to some extent in the West. The possible ways to reduce costs, among others, are strategic partnership and resources mobilization from other sources.

Second, accreditation-seeking institutions and / or program should critically follow guidelines to organize accreditation and diligently respond to the recommendations. The accreditation / the reward, the advice, and the rostering function by accreditation agencies provide essential insights to improve and maintain the quality and relevance of the PA programs, demonstrating the strategic use of the accreditation process.

Third, to improve and maintain the quality of the PA program, institutional capacity building and networking is imperative. It is also imperative to establish a National Association of PA schools and Networks of PA schools in Africa (Ethiopia) to promote the Africanization (Ethiopianization) in public administration education (Matsiliza 2020), which is consistent with pan-Africanism and AU's Agenda 2063. If cost is an issue, to some extent, they can organize conferences and dialogues online. The move should also give due attention to integrating global knowledge, suggesting EPAA and its partners, the Ethiopian PA universities, African PA higher education institutions, and stakeholders should work diligently toward this end.

Annexes

Annex 1. Three PA Curriculums during the Haile Selassie Regime

1951/52–1954/55 cohort	1957/58–1960/61 cohort	1967/68–1970/71 cohort
English Language (2)	English Language (3)	English Language Skills (2)
English Literature (4)	English Literature	College English (2)
French (4)	French IV, V	Amharic Language (3)
Philosophy (4)	Philosophy (2)	Logic
Ancient History	Ancient History	History of the World Civilizations (2)
Political Science (2)	Political Science	Principles of Government (2)
Public Speaking	Public Speaking (3)	Organization, Management, and Communication
Public Administration	Public Administration	Principles and Prob. of Public Admin. (2)
International Law and Relations	Introduction to Law and Relations	Labor Management and Government
Principles of Economic Policy	Fiscal Law and Financial Administration	Banking, Monetary, and Fiscal Policy
Counselor Affairs	History of Administrative laws	Municipal and Local administration (2)
Economic theory	Economic Geography	International Economics and Economic Development
Economics of Labor	Governmental Economics	Principles of Economics (2)
Economics	Economics	Introduction to Economics
Statistics	Statistics	Statistical Methods
Commerce and Industry	Accounting	Elementary Accounting
Introduction to Social Sciences	Introduction to Social Sciences	Introduction to Sociology
Book Keeping (2)	Bookkeeping	Development Administration
Greek History	Greek History	Public Personnel Administration (2)
Civil Law (2)	Administrative Law	Ethiopian Public Administration (3)

1951/52–1954/55 cohort	1957/58–1960/61 cohort	1967/68–1970/71 cohort
Survey of Africa	Public Administration (Comprehensive)	Politics and Government of African States (2)
Biology	Element and Techniques of Personnel Administration	Social Psychology
Process of Economic Growth	Personnel Management	Basic Mathematics
Survey of Asia	Comparative Government	Seminar on Selected Topics in PA
Roman History	Human Behavior	Public Law (3)
Survey of America	Algebra	Societies of Africa
Survey of Europe	Essay	Introduction to Life Science
History of Education (2)	Civil and Roman Law	Introduction to Geography
		Ethiopian Const. and Government
		Introduction to History of Ethiopia
		Introduction to Social Anthropology
		Urban Sociology
		Sociology of Religion
		People and Culture of Ethiopia
		Social and Cultural Change
		Race, Culture, and Society
		Selected Topics in Social Anthropology and Sociology (2)
		Seminar on Policy Development
		Seminar on Comparative Social Institutions

Sources: Complied from PA graduates' academic transcripts
The number in the bracket shows the frequency of the course

Annex 2. Three PA Curricula during the Derge Regime

1976/77–1979/80 Cohort. Major in Public Adm.	1986/87–1989/90 Cohort. Major in Public Adm.	1986/87–1989/90. Major in Management and Public Adm.
Freshman English (2)	Freshman English (2)	Freshman English (2)
Sophomore English	Sophomore English	Sophomore English
Political Economy (2)	Introduction to Political Economy	Introduction to Political Economy (2)
Introduction to Marxian Thoughts and Practice (2)	Foundation of Marxist-Leninist Philosophy (2)	Foundation of Marxist-Leninist Philosophy (2)
Public Personnel Management: Concepts and Issues	Personnel Management and Labor Relations	Personnel Management and Labor Relations
Techniques of Public Personnel Management	Public Personnel Administration	Personnel Management
Public Budgeting	Budgeting and Control	Budgeting and Control
Planning and Policy II	Theories and Pricing and Resources Allocation (2)	Theories and Pricing and Resources Allocation (2)
Organizational Planning and Policy	Public Policy Formulation	Policy Formulation and Administration
Basic Mathematics	Mathematics for Management	Mathematics for Management
Principles of Accounting	Principles of Accounting (2)	Principles of Accounting (2)
Organization and Management Analysis	Organization and Management	Organization and Management
Commercial and Organizational Law	Commercial Law	Commercial Law
Geography of Ethiopia	Introduction to the Geography of Ethiopia	Introduction to the Geography of Ethiopia
Introduction to Statistics	Elementary Quantitative Methods of Social Sciences (2)	Elementary Quantitative Methods of Social Sciences (2)
Introduction to Methods of Social Research	Research Methods	Research Methods
Research and Communication	Research Seminar on Ethiopian Public Administration	Organization, Management, and Seminar
Social Revolution	Social Revolution	Introduction to Management
Organization and Management of Public Enterprises	Organization and Management of Public Enterprises	Administrative Communication
Introduction to Public Administration (2)	Introduction to Public Administration	Principles of Marketing
Principles of Government	Principles of Management in Government Operation	Management Accounting
Comparative Political Systems	Comparative Political Systems	Materials Management

1976/77–1979/80 Cohort. Major in Public Adm.	1986/87–1989/90 Cohort. Major in Public Adm.	1986/87–1989/90. Major in Management and Public Adm.
Local Government and Regional Autonomy	Comparative Local Government	Management Information Systems
Government Accounting	Financial Management in Government Operation	Money and Banking
The Marxist Concept of State	Introduction to Scientific Communism	Financial Management
Marxist Analysis of Contemporary Political Issues	Management of Cooperatives	Managerial Statistics
Introduction to Marxist Thought and Practice I	Introduction to Management	General Psychology
Survey of Political Thought	Administrative Communication	Introduction to History of Ethiopia
Principles of Socialist Planning	Principles of Marketing	The Ethiopian Economy
Imperialism and Liberation Movement	Management Accounting	Physical Education (2)
Comparative Labor Relations	Materials Management	System Design and Analysis
Africa since the World War I	Management Information Systems	International Marketing
Political Ideas of the 3rd World	Money and Banking	Work Design, Measurement, and Compensation
African Political Systems	Financial Management	Operation Research
Introduction to International Relations	Managerial Statistics	Production Management
History of World Civilization	General Psychology	Managerial Economics
Introduction to Sciences	Introduction to History of Ethiopia	Financial Accounting
Post-1974 Political Development in Ethiopia	The Ethiopian Economy	Cost Accounting
Marxist Analysis of Pre-1974 Political Development in Ethiopia	Physical Education (2)	Project Analysis
Ethiopian Language	Law for Administration	Risk Management and Insurance
	Applied Administrative Management	International Marketing
	Municipal Management	

Source: Compiled from PA graduates' academic transcripts

ANNEXES

Annex 3. Three PA Curricula from 1993 to 2000

1993/94–1996/97 Cohort	1994/95–1998/99 Cohort	1996/97–1999/2000 Cohort
Name of BA: Major in Public Adm.	Name of BA: Major in Public Adm.	Name of BA: Major in Public Adm.
List of Courses and Frequency	List of Courses and Frequency	List of Courses and Frequency
Freshman English (2)	College English (2)	College English (2)
Sophomore English	Sophomore English	Sophomore English
Elementary Quantitative Methods for Social Sciences (2)	Quantitative Methods (2)	Quantitative Methods (2)
Physical Education (2)	Physical Education (2)	Physical Education (2)
Introduction to Philosophy	Philosophy (2)	Introduction to Philosophy
Survey of Ethiopian History and the Horn	Survey of Ethiopian History and the Horn (2)	Survey of Ethiopian History and the Horn (2)
Introduction to Management	Introduction to Management	Introduction to Management
Mathematics for Management	Mathematics for Management	Mathematics for Management
Principles of Accounting (2)	Principles of Accounting (2)	Principles of Accounting (2)
Theories of Pricing and Resources Allocation (2)	Theories of Pricing and Resources Allocation (2)	Theories of Pricing and Resources Allocation (2)
General Psychology	General Psychology	General Psychology
Administrative Communication	Business Communication	Business Communication
Managerial Statistics	Statistics for Management	Statistics for Management
The Ethiopian Economy	The Ethiopian Economy (2)	The Ethiopian Economy
Management Information System	Management Information System	Management Information System
Principles of Marketing	Principles of Marketing	Principles of Marketing
Personnel Management and Labor Relations	Human Resources Management	Human Resources Management
Organization and Management	Organization and Management	Organization and Management
Commercial Law	Business Law	Business Law
Management Accounting	Management Accounting	Management Accounting
Budgeting and Control	Budgeting and Control	Budgeting and Control
Research Methods	Research Methods	Research Methods
Materials Management	Materials Management	Materials Management
Introduction to Public Administration	Introduction to Public Administration	Introduction to Public Administration

1993/94–1996/97 Cohort	1994/95–1998/99 Cohort	1996/97–1999/2000 Cohort
Public Personnel Administration	Public Personnel Administration	Public Personnel Administration
Social Revolution	Social Revolution	Social Revolution
Law for Administrators	Law for Administrators	Law for Administrators
Organization and Management of Public Enterprises	Organization and Management of Public Enterprises	Organization and Management of Public Enterprises
Management of Cooperatives	Management of Cooperatives	Management of Cooperatives
Comparative Local Government	Comparative Local Government	Comparative Local Government
Financial Management in Government Operations	Financial Management in Government Operations	Financial Management in Government Operations
Applied Administrative Management	Applied Administrative Management	Applied Administrative Management
Research Seminar on Ethiopian Public Administration	Research Seminar on Ethiopian Public Administration	Research Seminar on Ethiopian Public Administration
Public Policy Formulation	Public Policy Formulation	Public Policy Formulation
Municipal Management	Municipal Management	Municipal Management
Comparative Political Systems	Comparative Political Systems	Comparative Political Systems
Financial Management	Financial Management	Financial Management
Introduction to Geography of Ethiopia and the Horn	Introduction to Computer Application in Business	Introduction to Computer Application in Business
Money and Banking	Introduction to Business	Introduction to Business
Introduction to Economics		Principles of Economics
Logic		Logic
Introduction to Political Science		
Introduction to Sociology		

Source: Complied for PA graduates' academic transcripts

Annex 4. BA in Development Administration Curriculum (ESCU), and BA in PA and Development Management Curriculum (AAU)

BA: Development Administration (1999/2000-2002/2003) ECSU	BA in PA and Development Management (2000/01-2004/05) AAU	BA in PA and Development Management 2004/05-2008/09 AAU
Study Skills, and Oral Communication (2)	College English (2)	College English (2)
Advance Writing	Sophomore English	Sophomore English
Introduction to Management	Introduction to Public & Development Administration (2)	Introduction to Public & Development Administration (2)
Introduction to Statistics	Quantitative Methods (2)	Quantitative Methods (2)
Statistics for Management	Statistics for Management	Statistics for Management
Mathematics for Management	Mathematics for Administrators (Management)	Mathematics for Management
Introduction to Public Administration	Development Administration	Development Administration
Development Communication	Administrative Communication	Administrative Communication
Principles of Accounting (2)	Principles of Accounting (2)	Principles of Accounting (2)
Public Finance	Public Finance and Taxation	Public Finance and Taxation
Government Budget and Control	Budgeting and Control	Budgeting and Control
Human Resource Management	Human Resources Management	Human Resources Management
Administration of Justice, Law and Order	Administrative Law	Administrative Law
Public Service and Labor Laws	Human Resources Administration	Public Personnel Administration
Organization and Management	Organization Theory and Behavior	Organization Theory and Behavior
Marketing	Principles of Marketing	Principles of Marketing
Management of Public Enterprises	Management and Organization of Public Enterprises	Management and Organization of Public Enterprises
Public Policy Formulation and Implementation	Public Policy Making and Analysis	Public Policy Making and Analysis
Project Management	Project Planning and Administration	Project Planning and Administration
Research Methodology	Research Methods	Research Methods

BA: Development Administration (1999/2000–2002/2003) ECSU	BA in PA and Development Management (2000/01–2004/05) AAU	BA in PA and Development Management 2004/05–2008/09 AAU
Seminar in Development Administration	Seminar in Public Administration (Senior Essay)	Seminar in Public Administration (Senior Essay)
Computer Skills	Introduction to Computer Application in Business	Introduction to Computer Application in Business
Managerial A	Public Sector Financial Administration	Public Sector Financial Administration
Commercial Law	Contract Law	Contract Law
Sociology for Development Administration	Introduction to Sociology	Introduction to Sociology
Introduction to Economics	Microeconomics (2)	Microeconomics (2)
Economics of Development	Principles of Economics	Principles of Economics
Rural Development	Local Government and Administration	Local Government and Administration
Urban Development	Urban Governance and Administration	Urban Governance and Administration
Strategic Management	Civic and Ethical Education	Civic and Ethical Education
Management Information System	Money and Banking	Money and Banking
Psychology for Development Administration	Entrepreneurship	Entrepreneurship
Managerial Accounting	Introduction to Politics and Government	Introduction to Politics and Government
Basic Mathematics	Introduction to Demography	Introduction to Demography
Introduction to Law	Logic	Introduction to Logic
Senior Essay	Introduction to Philosophy	Introduction to Philosophy
	Survey of Ethiopian History and the Horn (2)	Survey of Ethiopian History and the Horn (2)
	Physical Education (2)	Physical Education (2)
Materials Management	Materials Management	
Country Profile	Ethiopian Economy	

Annex 5. Harmonized BA Curriculum in Public Administration and Development Management

Name: All PA Universities (2013/14–2020/21)	Name: All PA Universities (2020/21)
Communicative English Skills	Communicative English Skills (2)
Basic Writing Skills	Basic Writing Skills
Introduction to Public Administration	Introduction to Public Administration
Theories and Politics of Development	Theories and Politics of Development
Introduction to Management+	Introduction to Management
Civics and Ethics	Moral and Ethical Education
Statistics for Management (2)	Statistics for Management (2)
Mathematics for Management	Mathematics for Management
Microeconomics	Microeconomics
Macroeconomics	Macroeconomics
Development Administration	Introduction to Development Management
Administrative Communication	Administrative Communication
Principles of Accounting (2)	Fundamentals of Accounting (2)
Public Finance and Taxation	Public Finance and Taxation
Public Budgeting and Financial Administration	Public Financial Administration and Budgeting
Local Government and Administration	Local Government and Administration
Urban Governance & Administration	Urban Governance and Administration
Human Resource Administration	Human Resource Management
Public personnel Administration	Public Personnel Administration
Organization Theory and Behaviors	Organization Theory and Behavior
Public Policy Formulation and Implementation	Public Policy Analysis and Implementation
Strategic Management+	Strategic Planning and Management°
Project Planning and Management	Project Planning and Management
Leadership and Change Management	Leadership and Change Management
Management of NGO's+	Governance and Management of Nongovernmental Organizations°
Management of Public Enterprises+	Governance and Management of Public Enterprises°
Public Service Delivery+	Public Service Delivery and E-Governance°
Introduction to Politics and Government	Introduction to Comparative Government and Politics

Name: All PA Universities (2013/14–2020/21)	Name: All PA Universities (2020/21)
Administrative Law	Administrative Law
Contract Law	Contract Law
Principles of Marketing	Principles of Marketing
Entrepreneurship	Entrepreneurship
Introduction to Computer Application	Computer Applications in Management
Introduction to Logic	Critical Thinking
Seminar in Public Administration (2)	Research Seminar on Public Administration (2)
Research Methods for Public Administration	Research Methods in Public Administration
	Introduction to Sociology
	Physical Fitness
	Geography of Ethiopia and the Horn
	Introduction to Sustainable Development
	Ethics in Public Administration
	Project Monitoring and Evaluation
	Inclusiveness
	Materials Management
	Economics
	Social Anthropology
	Global Trends
	Introduction to Emerging Technologies
	General Psychology
	Mathematics for Social Sciences
	Practical Attachment

Sources: Nationally Harmonized BA Curriculum in Public Administration and Development Management (AAU, 2013)

Annex 6. BA Curricula Major in Governance and Development Management/Studies, and BA Major in Development Management

BA in GaDS (HU) (2007–2012)	All Uni BA in GaDs (2013–2020/21)	All Uni BA in GaDs (2020/21)	ECSU BA in Dev't Mgt (2015–2019)
Communicative English Skill	Communicative English	Communicative English Skills	Basic English
Development Theories and Practice	Development Theories and Practices	Development Theories and Practices	Principles of Development Management
Public Policy Making and Analysis	Public Policy Making and Analysis	Public Policy Making and Analysis	Public Policy Management
Development Economics	Development Economics	Development Economics	Development Economics
Human Resource Governance and Development	Human Resource Governance and Development	Human Resources Management	Human Resources Management
Development Project Planning and Management	Project Planning and Management	Project Planning and Management	Project Management
Organizational Management and Leadership	Organizational Management and Leadership	Organizational Leadership and Management	Theories and Practices of Leadership
Gender and Development	Gender and Development	Gender and Development	Population, Gender, and Development
Administrative Law	Administrative Law	Administrative Law	Law for Managers
Introduction to Logic	Introduction to Logic	Logic and Critical Thinking	Introduction to Logic (2019)
Introduction to Ethics	Civic and Ethics	Moral and Civics Education	Ethics and Public Service Delivery
Research Methods in Social Science	Research Methods in Social Science	Research Methods in Social Science	Research Methodology
Seminar on Development Policies and Practices in Ethiopia	Seminar on Development Policies and Practices in Ethiopia	Seminar on Development Policies and Practices in Ethiopia	Seminar in Development Management
Senior Essay	Senior Essay	Senior Essay	Senior Essay
	Basic Writing skills	Communicative English Skills	Advance Writing
	Introduction to Management	Introduction to Management	Introduction to Management
	Introduction to Public Administration	Introduction to Public Administration	Principles of Public Administration

BA in GaDS (HU) (2007–2012)	All Uni BA in GaDs (2013–2020/21)	All Uni BA in GaDs (2020/21)	ECSU BA in Dev't Mgt (2015–2019)
	Introduction to Information Communication Technology	Introduction to Emerging Technologies	Computer Skills
	Entrepreneurship and Development	Entrepreneurship	Entrepreneurship and Enterprise Development (2019)
Quantitative Methods for Development	Quantitative Research Methods	Introduction to Research Methods	Basic and Applied Statics for Management
African Politics and International Relations	Governance and International Relations of Africa	African Politics and International Relations	Governance and Democracy (2019)
Introduction to International Relation	Introduction to International Relations	International Relations and Organizations	Basic Accounting and Accounting Reforms (2015)
Introduction to Politics and Governance	Introduction to Politics and Governance	Introduction to Politics and Government	Principles of Marketing
Constitutionalism and Public Law	Constitutional Law and Constitutionalism	Constitutional Law and Constitutionalism	Administrative Communication
Comparative Governance and Political System	Comparative Government and Political Systems	Comparative Government and Political Systems	Materials Management
Urban Governance and Municipal Management	Urban Governance and Municipal Management	Urban Governance and Municipal Management	Management Information System
International Political Economy	International Political Economy	International Political Economy	General Psychology
International Law and Organization	Public International Law and Organizations	Public International Law	Strategic Management
Political System and Governance in Ethiopia	Political Systems and Governance in Ethiopia	Political Systems and Governance in Ethiopia	Sociology for Development Management
Peace Building and Conflict Management	Conflict Management and Peace Building	Conflict Management and Peace Building	Public Finance and Taxation
Regional Growth and Local Development	Regional Growth and Local Development	Regional Growth and Local Development	Macroeconomics
Federalism: Focus on Ethiopia	Federalism and Local Government in Ethiopia	Federalism and Local Government in Ethiopia	
Human Right and Democracy	Human Rights and Humanitarian Assistance	Human Rights and Humanitarian Assistance	Disaster and Risk Management
Political Thought	Political Theories	Political Thought (2)	Microeconomics

ANNEXES

BA in GaDS (HU) (2007–2012)	All Uni BA in GaDs (2013–2020/21)	All Uni BA in GaDs (2020/21)	ECSU BA in Dev't Mgt (2015–2019)
Environment and Natural Resource Governance	Environment and Development	Environment and Natural Resource Management	
	Development Finance	Development Finance	Government Budgeting and Expenditure Management
	Rural Development	Rural Development	Rural and Urban Development
	Ethiopian Land Law and Development	Land Governance in Ethiopia	Organizational Behavior
	Population and Development	Population and Development	Basic and Applied Mathematics for Management
Society and Challenge Management		Theories and Practice of Governance	
Development Issues and Challenges in Developing Countries		Development Planning and Management	
Seminar on Comparative Development Policies and Practices		Governance and Institutional Reform	
Community Mobilization and Development		Foreign Policy and Diplomacy: Ethiopian Focus	
Financial Management in Government		Introduction to Multiculturalism	
Institution and Public Sector Reform		Community Development	
Foreign Policy and Diplomacy		Inclusiveness	
Media, Public Opinion, and Democracy		General Psychology	
Globalization and Development		Geography of Ethiopia and the Horn	
		Mathematics for Social Science	
		Global Affairs	
		Introduction to Economics	
		Social Anthropology	
		History of Ethiopia and the Horn	
		Physical Fitness	

Annex 7. MA and PhD Curricula

MA MA in Public Administration / Management Cluster	
MA in Public Administration (2005–2012) (AAU)	**MA in Public Management and Policy (MPMP) (2012–) (AAU)**
– Principles of Public Administration	– Pedagogy
– Theories of Public Organization	– Theories of Public Organization
– Research Methods in Public Administration	– Research Methods in Public Management
– Public Personnel Administration	– Principles of Public Management
– Public Budgeting and Finance	– Public Finance, Budgeting, and Intergovernmental Relations
– Public Policy Making and Analysis	– Public Policy Analysis*
– Program Design, Implementation, and Evaluation	– Policy and Institutional Reforms*
– Development Management, Politics, and Administration	– Social Policy Analysis*
– Elective courses and special topic for 1 credit hour	– Development Management and Policy**
– Master's Thesis	– Sustainable Development Management**
	– Program Management in the Public Sector**
	– Local Governance and Development**
	– MA Thesis
MA in Public Management (PM) (2014–18) (ECSU)	**MA in Public Management (PM) (2018–) (ECSU**
– Public Management: Principles and Comparison	– Principles and Theories of Public Management
– Ethiopian Public Administration, Governance, and Ethics	– Management Information System (MIS)
– Research Methodology for Public Managers	– Advanced Research Methodology
– Organizational Behavior	– Organizational Behavior
– Resource Management in Public Organizations	– Human Resources Management
– Public Policy Formulation and Implementation	– Public Policy Formulation and Analysis
– Strategic Management in the Public Sector	– Public Sector Strategic Management
– Development Theories and Strategies	– Development Theories and Strategies
– Public Sector Project Management	– Project Planning and Management
– Seminar in Public Management	– Seminar in Public Management
– MA's Thesis	– Public Finance and Budgeting
	– MA Thesis

MA MA in Public Administration / Management Cluster

MA in Public Administration (2020–) Assosa	MA in Public Mgt and Policy Development (2018–) Hawassa
– Theories and Practices of Public Administration	– Theories of Public Management and Policy Development
– Organization Theory and Behavior	– Public Management and Policy
– Advanced Research Methods	– Qualitative and Quantitative Research Methods
– Public Finance and Budgeting	– Public Finance and Budgeting
– Leadership and Governance	– Human Resource Management and Leadership
– Public Policy Analysis and Implementation	– Public Policy Analysis
– Development Administration	– Transformative Social Policy for Development: Ethiopia
– Local and Urban Governance and Administration	– Public Policy Development and Management
– Project Planning and Administration	– Public Project and Program Management
– Federalism and Intergovernmental Relations	– Community Development and Governance
– Advanced Administrative Law	– Poverty and Development Policy
– Peace Building and Conflict Management	– MA Thesis
– MA Thesis	

*= Specialization in Public Policy Studies, **=Specialization in Development Management

MA Curricula in Development and Public Policy Cluster

MA in Development Policy (2019) (ECSU)	MA in Policy Analysis (2019) ECSU
– Introduction to Public Policy Studies	– Introduction to Policy Studies
– Development Theories, Policies and Issues	– Fundamentals of Social Policy
– Fundamentals of Social Policy	– Statistics for Policy Analysts
– Advanced Research Methods	– Research Methodology for Policy Analysts
– Ethiopian Public Administration, Governance, and Ethics	– Ethiopian Public Administration Governance, and Ethics
– Institutions and Economic Development	– Economic Theories: Policies and Issues
– Management of Development Programs and Projects	– Evaluation Tools and Techniques
– Local Governance and Development	– Quantitative Data Analysis
– Environmental Management and Sustainable Development	– Policy Analysis
– Development Policy Analysis and Evaluation	– Policy Implementation and Governance
– Public Finance, Budgeting, and Intergovernmental Relations	– Policy Analysis Workshop
– Development Policy Seminar	– Comparative Public Policy Seminar
– MA Thesis	– MA Thesis

MA Curricula in Development and Public Policy Cluster

MA in Public Policy Studies (2019) (ECSU)	MA in Social Policy (2019) (ECSU)
- Introduction to Public Policy Studies	- Fundamentals of Social Policy
- Development Theories, Policies, and Practices	- Introduction to Public Policy Studies
- Ethiopian Public Administration, Governance, & Ethics	- Ethiopian Public Administration, Governance and Ethics
- Advanced Research Methods	- Advanced Research Methods
- Public Policy and Federalism	- Economics for Social Policy
- Policy Implementation and Governance	- Urbanization and Social Capital
- Policy Evaluation and Innovation	- Sociology of Development
- Fundamentals of Social Policy	- Social Policy Analysis
- Public-Private Partnership Policy	- Social Policy Evaluation
- Comparative Public Policy and Globalization	- Comparative Social Policy and Administration
- Seminar on Ethiopian Public Policies	- Seminar on Ethiopian Social Policies
- MA Thesis	- MA Thesis
MA in Social Security Management (2019) (ECSU)	**MA in Peace and Security (2019) ECSU**
- The Socioeconomics of Social Protection	- Introduction to Peace and Security
- Public Sector Economics	- Conflict Resolution and Peace-building
- Applied Project in Social Protection	- Culture of Peace: Identity and Culture
- Advanced Research Methodology	- Research Methods in Governance and Dev't
- Social Protection Financing	- Gender, Conflict and Peace-Building
- Disaster Risk Management	- Federalism and Conflict Resolution
- Quantitative Social Protection Analysis	- Cyber Security
- Strategic Interventions to Social Protection Management	- Hydro-Politics and Security in Africa
- Social Protection Administration and Policy Implementation	- Ethiopian Public Administration, Governance, and Ethics
- Comparative Analysis of Social Protection	- Regional and Global Peace and Security
- Project Planning and Management	- Seminar in Peace and Security Studies
- MA Thesis	- MA Thesis

MA Curricula in Public Financial Management and Leadership and Governance Clusters

MA in Public Financial Management (2018–) (OSU)	MA in Public Financial Management (PM) (2019–) (ECSU)
– Financial Management of Government and NFPs	– Financial Management of Government and Nonprofit Organizations
– Public Expenditure Management and Control	– Public Expenditure Management and Control
– Banking and Financial Institutions Management	– Public Procurement Principles and Practices
– Customs Management Theory and Practice	– Customs Management Theory and Practice
– International Public Financial Management	– International Public Financial Management
– Public Sector Economics	– Public Sector Economics
– Public Sector Accounting and Reporting	– Public Sector Auditing and Assurance
– Research Methods	– Advanced Research Methodology (2)
– Advanced Taxation	– Tax Design and Administration
– Project Management and Financing	– Project Management
– Strategic Management for Public and Nonprofit Organizations	– MA Thesis
– Public Sector Auditing	
– MA Thesis	

MA in Leadership and Governance (2019) ECSU	MA in Leadership and Change Mgt (2018) OSU
– Leadership and Management Concepts, Theories, and Practices	– Philosophies and Models of Leadership
– Development Issues / Theories and the Ethiopian Situation	– Management of Change and Innovation
– Strategic Management for Leadership	– Strategic Management
– Public Administration and Governance for Leadership	– Macroeconomic environment and Public Policy for Leadership
– Leading People and Managing Resources and Operations	– Organizational Behavior
– Legal Frameworks for Leadership	– Contemporary Legal Matters
– Research Methodology for Leadership	– Research Methodology
– Leadership Ethics and Service Delivery	– Managing Finance for Leadership
– Public Policy for Leadership	– Advanced Project Management
– International Relations and Globalizations	– Change and Performance Management
– Academic Writing and Seminar for Leadership	– Seminar in Leadership and Change Management
– Leadership and Mgt Concepts, Theories and Practices	– MA Thesis
– Transformational Leadership	
– MA Thesis	

MA Curricula in Development Management and Governance Cluster

MA in Development Management (2016) AU	MA in Development Management (2015) OSU
- Leadership and Change Management	- Development Management and Leadership
- Principles of Development Management	- Social Policy and Development
- Development Communication and Ethics	- Public Finance and Development
- Gender and Development	- Public Administration and Governance
- Development Policy Formulation and Evaluation	- Development Economics and Policies
- Financial Accounting and Management	- Contemporary Legal Matters
- Advanced Research Methods	- Research Methodology
- Social Entrepreneurship for Sustainable Livelihood	- Environment and Development
- Project Planning and Management	- Developmental Project Planning and Analysis
- Management of Local Development and Resource Mobilization	- Political Economy in Developing Countries
- Seminar in Development Management	- Advanced Econometrics
- MA Thesis	- MA Thesis

MA in Development Management (2019–) (ESUC)	MA in Governance and Development (2019–) (ECSU)
- Development Theories and Practices	- Governance and Democracy
- Development Management and Organizations	- Pastoralism and Environmental Governance
- Principles of Public Administration and Governance	- Comparative Constitutions and Federalism
- Disaster and Risk Management	- Regional Integration and Globalization
- Finance and Development Management in Public Sector	- Conflict Resolution and Security Governance
- Rural-Urban Development	- Development Policies and Strategies
- Development Research Methods	- Research Methods in Governance and Development
- Sustainable Development Management	- Gender and Entrepreneurship
- Development Project Management	- Public Administration and Leadership
- Internship in Development Management	- Seminar in Governance and Development
- Development Economics	- Project Planning and Management
- MA Thesis	- MA Thesis

MA Curricula in Development Management and Governance Cluster

MA in Development Management (2019) (HU)	MA in Governance and Development (2019) (HU)
- Theory and Practice of Development	- Political Theories
- Livelihood Improvement and Poverty Reduction in Ethiopia	- Theories of Governance and Development
- Urban Development and Regional Planning	- International Political Economy of Development and Underdevelopment
- Development Policy and Management	- Decentralization and Local Governance
- Population, Environment, and Development	- Society, State, and Globalization
- Development Project Planning and Management	- Public Policy Making and Analysis
- Advanced Research Methods	- Advanced Research Methodology
- Development Finance	- Public Management and Organizational Development
- Seminar on Emerging Issues in Development Management: Thoughts, Debates, policies and experiences	- Seminar on Governance and Development Issues in Ethiopia
- MA Thesis	- Environmental Governance
	- Labor, Social Movements, and Development
	- Governance and Agrarian Transformation
	- Governance and Institutional Reforms [elective course]
	- Development Finance [elective course]
	- MA Thesis

PA PhD Program Curricula

PhD in Public Management and Policy (AU)	PhD in Public Management (ECSU)
- Advanced Theories of Public Management and Organizational Behavior	- Public Sector Management
- Public Finance and Budgeting	- Comparative Public Sector Management: Analytical Tools and Strategies
- Comparative Public Policy	- Public Policy Making, Implementation and Analysis
- Research Method (2)	- Advanced Research Methodology (2)
- Urban and Local Governance	- Knowledge Area Development Module (Seminar)
- Human Resource Management	- Dissertation
- Dissertation	

PA PhD Program Curricula

PhD Program in Federal Studies (AU)	PhD in Public Financial Management (ECSU)
- Theories and Praxis on Peace, Federalism, and Human Rights	- Theories and Models of Public Finance
- Federalism and Nation Building in Multi-Ethnic Society	- Public Budget and Fiscal Policy
- Comparative Federal Political System	- Econometrics for Public Finance Using STATA and E. Views
- Advanced Research Methodology	- Advanced Research Methodology (2)
- Seminar on Conflict, Governance, and Human Rights in the Horn of Africa	- Knowledge Area Development (Seminar)
- Federalism and Decentralization in the Horn of Africa	- Dissertation
- Dissertation	

PhD in Policy and Development Studies (Hawassa)

- Advanced Policy Making and Analysis
- Sustainable Agriculture and Food Security
- Global Political-Economy and International Trade Policy
- Advanced Research Methodology
- Seminar on Macroeconomic Policy
- Governance, Conflict Analysis and Management
- Evaluation of Development Policy, Program and Projects
- Dissertation

Annex 8. International Commission on Accreditation of Public Administration Education and Training (ICAPA) Self-Assessment Guide Document

1. *Program Contact Information*
   A. Name of the Department/School/University/Training Institution Offering the Program
   B. Head of the School/University/Training Institution (Name, Title, Address, Phone, Fax, E-Mail)
   C. Program Leader/Representative/Coordinator (Name, Title, Address, Phone, Fax, E-Mail)
   D. Program Leader/Representative/Coordinator (Name, Title, Address, Phone, Fax, E-Mail)
   E. Accreditation Representative/Coordinator (Name, Title, Address, Phone, Fax, E-mail)
2. **Overview of the Program Seeking Accreditation Review**
   A. Level of activity or program accreditation
      - Bachelor level
      - Master's level
      - PhD level
      - Certificate level
      - Training program level
   B. **Full title of the program**
   C. **Website of the program**
   D. Launch date of the program (please indicate the year)
   E. Statement of program mission and objectives (identify the program's mission statement, goals, and objectives)
   F. Main focus of the program (such as Public Administration, Public Affairs, Public Management, Public Policy, Local Government, etc.)
   G. Existing accreditation status (please specify the name of any and all accreditation bodies—national, regional, public, private, and / or nonprofit—the type of accreditation received, as well as the date of issuance and validity period)
   H. Number of students enrolled in the program (average number of full time and average number of part time students enrolled per year since the program's launch, or over the past five years)
   I. **Origins of the program and its history** *(please briefly review the origins and evolution of the program)*
   J. National system of higher education (please provide a brief summary of the organization of public and / or private higher education system in the nation, and how this impacts public administration education and training)
   K. Program and its environment (if necessary, please provide a brief summary of the uniqueness of the program and the specific environment in which the program functions)
3. Self-Assessment on Standards
   Standard 1: Public Service Commitment
   A. Program design
   B. Research involvement
   C. Service involvement
   D. Contribution to the discipline
   Standard 2: Advocacy of Public Interest Values
   A. Reflection of public interest values in curriculum
   B. Exemplary function
   C. Community consultation
   D. Communication
   E. Information availability to the public

F. Impact on the community
G. Grievances

Standard 3: Combining Scholarship, Practice, and Community Service
A. Program basis
B. Community engagement activities
C. Practical experience
D. Program level

Standard 4: The Faculty Are Central
A. Human resources management (HRM) system
B. Program faculty
C. Faculty review
D. Number of core faculty / staff
E. Faculty / staff remuneration

Standard 5: Inclusiveness is at the Heart of the Program
A. Social and cultural diversity
B. Multidisciplinary

Standard 6: A Curriculum That Is Purposeful and Responsive
A. Curriculum
B. Program goals and objectives
C. Educational strategy
D. Program coherence and consistency
E. Strategic planning process
F. Assessment
G. Delivery consistency

Standard 7: Adequate Resources Are Critical
A. Program responsibility and administration
B. Program budget and financial structure
C. Facilities
D. Student services

Standard 8: Balancing Collaboration and Competition
A. Benchmarking
B. Program admission
C. Student success

References

Aalen, L. (2020). The Revolutionary Democracy of Ethiopia: A Wartime Ideology Both Shaping and Shaped by Peacetime Policy Needs. *Government and Opposition*, 55(4), 653–668.

AAU (2010). PhD in Public Management and Policy Curriculum. Addis Ababa University.

AAU (2012). MA in Public Management and Policy Curriculum. Addis Ababa University.

AAU (2013). Nationally Harmonized Modular Curriculum for Bachelor of Arts Degree (BA) in Public Administration and Development Management (PADM). Addis Ababa University.

Abbink, J. (2006). Discomfiture of Democracy? The 2005 Election Crisis in Ethiopia and Its Aftermath. *African Affairs*, 105(419), 173–199.

Abbink, J. (2011). Ethnic-Based Federalism and Ethnicity in Ethiopia: Reassessing the Experiment after 20 Years. *Journal of Eastern African Studies*, 5(4), 596–618.

Adamu, A. Y., & Addamu, A. M. (2012). Quality Assurance in Ethiopian Higher Education: Procedures and Practices. *Procedia-Social and Behavioral Sciences*, 69, 838–846.

African Union. (2014a). Agenda 2063 African Union Commission Archives. https://au.int/en/agenda2063.

African Union. (2014b). AU Outlook on Education Report. Continental Report. https://reliefweb.int/sites/reliefweb.int/files/resources/au_outlook_continental_english_2014_w.pdf.

African Union (2016). Continental Education Strategy for Africa 2016–2025. https://au.int/sites/default/files/documents/29958-doc-cesa_-_english-v9.pdf.

Albareda-Tiana, S., Ruíz-Morales, J., Azcárate, P., Valderrama-Hernández, R., & Múñoz, J. M. (2020). The EDINSOST Project: Implementing the Sustainable Development Goals at University Level. In: *Universities as Living Labs for Sustainable Development* (pp. 193–210). Springer, Cham.

Aleixo, A. M., Azeiteiro, U. M., & Leal, S. (2020). Are the Sustainable Development Goals Being Implemented in the Portuguese Higher Education Formative Offer? *International Journal of Sustainability in Higher Education* 21(2), 336–352.

Angaw, K. W. (2020). Catch-Up Trails: Public Administration Education and Professionalization Trajectories in Ethiopia. In: Debela, B. K., Bouckaert G., Warota A. M., and Gemechu, T. D. (eds), *Public Administration in Ethiopia: Case Studies and Lessons for Sustainable Development* (pp. 591–611). Leuven University Press, Lueven.

Ansell, C., Sørensen, E., & Torfing, J. (2021). The COVID-19 Pandemic as a Game Changer for Public Administration and Leadership? The Need for Robust Governance Responses to Turbulent Problems. *Public Management Review*, 23(7), 949–960.

Bach, J. N. (2011). Abyotawi Democracy: Neither Revolutionary nor Democratic, a Critical Review of EPRDF's Conception of Revolutionary Democracy in Post-1991 Ethiopia. *Journal of Eastern African Studies*, 5(4), 641–663.

Bach, J. N. (2014). EPRDF's Nation-Building: Tinkering with Convictions and Pragmatism. *Cadernos de Estudos Africanos*, (27).

Bertels, J., Bouckaert, G., & Jann, W. (2020). The Survey: A Long-Distance Conversation about the Future of Public Administration in Europe. In: Bouckaert and Jann (eds), *European Perspectives for Public Administration: The Way Forward* (pp. 43–70). Leuven University Press, Leuven.

Bouckaert, G. (2020). From Public Administration in Utopia to Utopia in Public Administration. In: Bouckaert and Jann, *European Perspectives for Public Administration* (pp. 71–84

Bouckaert, G., Jann, W., Maron, F., Ongaro, E., & Sahraoui, S. (2019). Conclusion: EGPA, EPPA and the Future of Public Administration in Europe. In: Ongaro, E. (ed.), *Public Administration in Europe* (pp. 355–361). Palgrave Macmillan, Cham.

Brans, M., & Coenen, L. (2016). The Europeanization of Public Administration Teaching. *Policy and Society*, 35(4), 333–349.

Breaux, D. A., Clynch, E. J., & Morris, J. C. (2003). The Core Curriculum Content of NASPAA-Accredited Programs: Fundamentally Alike or Different? *Journal of Public Affairs Education*, 9(4), 259–273.

Brintnall, M. (2015). Some Reflections on What International Standards Really Will Do. In: Rosenbaum, A. (ed.), *In Quest of Excellence: Approaches to Enhancing the Quality of Public Administration Education and Training* (pp. 130–138). United Nations, NIPSAcee Press.

CAPPA (Canadian Association of Program in Public Administration) (nd): https:// cappa.ca/en/ (last consulted, 31/03/2022).

Crossman, P. (1999). *Endogenisation and African Universities: Initiatives and Issues in the Quest for Plurality in the Human Sciences; A Report on a Policy-Forming Research Project Commissioned by the Flemish University Council (Vl. IR) with the Support of the Belgian Administration for Development (ABOS)*. Belgian Administration for Development Co-Operation.

Daemen, H., & van der Krogt, T. (2008). Four Functions of International Accreditation: The Case of EAPAA and Public Administration in the Netherlands. In: Jenei, G., and Mike, K. (eds), *Public Administration and Public Policy Degree Programs in Europe: The Road from Bologna* (pp. 25–38). NISPAcee Press, Slovak Republic.

Daniels, M. R., & Johansen, E. (1985). Role of Accreditation in the Development of Public Administration as a Profession: a Theoretical and Empirical Assessment. *Public Administration Quarterly*, 8(4), 419–441.

Debela, B. K., and Troupin, S. (2020). Transforming Ethiopian Public Administration for Sustainable Development: The Impact of Organizational Proliferation and Policy Coordination on Access to Drinking Water. In: Scott, G., and Wallis, M. (eds). *Transformation of Public Administration in Africa* (pp. 72–101). African Association for Public Administration and Management.

Debela, B. K., Bouckaert, G., Warota, M. A., and Gemechu, D. T. (2020a). Introduction to Public Administration in Ethiopia: Case Studies and Lessons for Sustainable Development. In Debela, Bouckaert, Warota, and Gemechu, *Public Administration in Ethiopia* (pp. 665–689).

Debela, B. K., Bouckaert, G., Warota, M. A., and Gemechu, D. T. (2020b). Conclusions and Implications. In: Debela, Bouckaert, Warota, and Gemechu, (eds). *Public Administration in Ethiopia* (pp. 691–699).

Develtere, P., Huyse, H., & Van Ongevalle, J. (2021). *International Development Today. International Cooperation Development Today. A Radical Shift towards a Global Paradigm*. Leuven, Leuven University Press.

ECSU (2017). Doctor of Philosophy (PhD) in Public Financial Management Curriculum, Ethiopian Civil Service University.

ECSU (2018). Doctor of Philosophy (PhD) in Public Management Curriculum, Ethiopian Civil Service University.

ECSU (2019). MA in Policy Analysis Curriculum, Ethiopian Civil Service University.

FDRE (2009). Higher Education Proclamation no. 650/2019. Negarit Gazeta, Addis Ababa.

FDRE (2019). Revised Higher Education Proclamation no. 1152/2019. Negarit Gazeta, Addis Ababa.

Federal Democratic Republic Government of Ethiopia (1994). Education and Training Policy. https://www.cmpethiopia.org/media/education_and_training_policy_ethiopia_1994.

Finnveden, G., Newman, J., & Verhoef, L. A. (2019). Sustainable Development and Higher Education: Acting with a Purpose. *Sustainability*, *11*(14), 3831.

Fleacă, E., Fleacă, B., & Maiduc, S. (2018). Aligning Strategy with Sustainable Development Goals (SDGs): Process Scoping Diagram for Entrepreneurial Higher Education Institutions (HEIs). *Sustainability*, *10*(4), 1032.

Franco, I., Saito, O., Vaughter, P., Whereat, J., Kanie, N., & Takemoto, K. (2019). Higher Education for Sustainable Development: Actioning the Global Goals in Policy, Curriculum and Practice. *Sustainability Science*, *14*(6), 1621–1642.

Gebru, G. S., Hondeghem, A., and Broucker, B. (2020). Institutional Autonomy of Ethiopian Public Universities: An Application of the European University Autonomy Scorecard Methodology. In: Debela, Bouckaert, Warota, and Gemechu, *Public Administration in Ethiopia* (pp. 531–563).

Grano, C., & Prieto, V. C. (2020). Sustainable Development Goals in Higher Education. In *26th IJCIEOM–International Joint Conference on Industrial Engineering and Operations Management, Rio de Janeiro*.

Gutema, M. M. (2020). The Analysis of the Gadaa System in Comparison to Global Democracy. In Debela, Bouckaert, Warota, and Gemechu, *Public Administration in Ethiopia* (pp. 279–393).

Guy, M. E., & Stillman, R. (2016). On NASPAA Accreditation: Fred Was Right … but for the Wrong Reason. *Journal of Public Affairs Education*, *22*(2), 303–312.

Hagmann, T., & Abbink, J. (2011). Twenty Years of Revolutionary Democratic Ethiopia, 1991 to 2011. *Journal of Eastern African Studies*, *5*(4), 579–595.

HAQAA Consortium (2018a). African Standards and Guidelines for Quality Assurance in Higher Education (ASG-QA), https://haqaa.aau.org/activities/african-standards-and-guidelines-for-quality-assurance-asg-qa/.

HAQAA Consortium (2018b). Mapping of the Existing Standards and Guidelines in Quality Assurance in African Countries, *and a Brief Introduction to Quality Assurance in the European Higher Education Area*. https://haqaa.aau.org/wp-content/uploads/2018/05/ASG-QA-existing-standards_final_EN.pdf.

Haug, G. (2003). Quality Assurance/Accreditation in the Emerging European Higher Education Area: A Possible Scenario for the Future. *European Journal of Education*, 38(3), 229–240.

Hawassa University (HU) (2013). Nationally Harmonized Modular Curriculum for Bachelor of Arts Degree (BA) in Governance and Development Studies (GaDS). Hawassa University.

Hayward, F. (2006). Quality Assurance and Accreditation of Higher Education in Africa. In: *Conference Paper on Higher Education Reform in Francophone Africa: Understanding the Keys of Success*. Ouagadougou, Burkina Faso.

Higher Education Relevance and Quality Agency (HERQA) (2007). Institutional Quality Audit, Guidance on Focus Area Thresholds. HERQA QA01/07/V1. www.herqa.edu.et.

Holmes, M. H. (2020). The Accreditation Process. In: McDonald III, B. D., & Hatcher, W. (eds), *The Public Affairs Faculty Manual: A Guide to the Effective Management of Public Affairs Programs* (98-109). Routledge, London.

Jabes, J. (2008). On the Way to Bologna: Developments in Public Policy Programs in Europe. In: Jenei Mike, *Public Administration and Public Policy Degree Programs* (pp 11–24).

Jiru, A. C. (2020). Outcomes and Challenges of the 1994 Ethiopian Education and Training Policy Reform. In: Debela, Bouckaert, Warota, and Gemechu, *Public Administration in Ethiopia* (pp. 665–689).

Katsamunska, P. (2015). Government Accreditation and Oversight of Academic Public Administration Programs: The Case of Bulgaria. In Rosenbaum, A. (ed), *In Quest of Excellence*: (pp. 85–97).

Ketlhoilwe, M. J., Silo, N., & Velempini, K. (2020). Enhancing the Roles and Responsibilities of Higher Education Institutions in Implementing the Sustainable Development Goals. In: Nhamo, G., & Mjimba, V. (eds), *Sustainable Development Goals and Institutions of Higher Education* (pp. 121–130). Springer, Cham.

Klun, M., & Reichard, C. (2019). Accreditation in European Public Administration. In: Ongaro, *Public Administration in Europe* (pp. 345–354).

Korhonen-Kurki, K., Koivuranta, R., Kuitto, V., Pietikäinen, J., Schönach, P., & Soini, K. (2020). Towards Realising SDGs in the University of Helsinki. In: Nhamo & Mjimba, *Sustainable Development Goals and Institutions of Higher Education* (pp. 15–29).

Kuhlmann, E., Dussault, G., & Correia, T. (2021). Global Health and Health Workforce Development: What to Learn from COVID-19 on Health Workforce Preparedness and Resilience. *International Journal of Health Planning and Management*, 36(S1), 5–8.

Leal Filho, W., Manolas, E., & Pace, P. (2015). The Future we Want: Key Issues on Sustainable Development in Higher Education after Rio and the UN Decade of Education for Sustainable Development. *International Journal of Sustainability in Higher Education*, 16(1).

Lefort, R. (2012). Free Market Economy, "Developmental State" and Party-State Hegemony in Ethiopia: The Case of the "Model Farmers." *Journal of Modern African Studies*, 50(4), 681–706.

Lubinescu, E. S., Ratcliff, J. L., & Gaffney, M. A. (2001). Two Continuums Collide: Accreditation and Assessment. *New Directions for Higher Education, 2001*(113), 5–21.

Mascio, F. D., Natalini, A., & Cacciatore, F. (2020). Public Administration and Creeping Crises: Insights from COVID-19 Pandemic in Italy. *American Review of Public Administration, 50*(6–7), 621–627.

Matsiliza, N. S. (2020). Decolonisation in the Field of Public Administration: The Responsiveness of the Scholarship of Teaching and Learning. *Teaching Public Administration, 38*(3), 295–312.

McFarland, L. (2015). Quality Assurance in the International Market for Public Affairs Education. In Rosenbaum, *In Quest of Excellence* (pp. 75–84).

Mengesha, G. H., & Common, R. (2007). Public Sector Capacity Reform in Ethiopia: A Tale of Success in Two Ministries? *Public Administration and Development, 27* (5), 367–80.

Ministry of Education (2020). Ethiopian Education Development Roadmap (2018–30). An Integrated Executive Summary. Ministry of Education, Education Strategy Center (ESC).

Ministry of Education (MOE). (2002). Education Sector Development Program II (ESDP-II) Program Action Plan (PAP). Addis Ababa, FDRE.

Ministry of Education (MOE). (2005). Education Sector Development Program III (ESDP-IV) (2005–2010). Unpublished report, Addis Ababa, FDRE.

Ministry of Education (MOE). (2010). Education Sector Development Program IV(ESDP-IV) (2010–2014). Unpublished report, Addis Ababa, FDRE.

Mishra, R. K. (2015). Standards for Public Administration Education and Training in Selected Asian Countries. In: Rosenbaum, *In Quest of Excellence* (pp. 221–258).

NASPAA (Network of Schools of Public Policy, Affairs, and Administration) (nd) https://www.naspaa.org/accreditation (last consulted, 31/03/2022).

Nemec, J. (2008). Accreditation Processes in Slovakia and Neighbouring Countries in Central Europe: Current Problems and Possible Improvements. In: Jenei Mike, *Public Administration and Public Policy Degree Programs in Europe* (pp: 39–53).

Newcomer, K., & Allen, H. (2015). Public Administration Education: Adding Value in the Public Service. In: Rosenbaum, *In Quest of Excellence* (pp. 43–59).

Nhamo, G. (2020). Higher Education and the Energy Sustainable Development Goal: Policies and Projects from University of South Africa. In: Nhamo & Mjimba *Sustainable Development Goals and Institutions of Higher Education* (pp. 31–48).

Nhamo, G., & Mjimba, V. (2020). The Context: SDGs and Institutions of Higher Education. In: Nhamo & Mjimba *Sustainable Development Goals and Institutions of Higher Education* (pp. 1–13).

Olkaba, T. (2016). Globalization and Its Impact on Higher Education Policy in Ethiopia. Doctoral Thesis. University of South Africa. https://stemedhub.org/resources/4359.

Ongaro, E. (2019). Introduction: The Past and the Future of a Community at the Heart of the Administrative Sciences. In: Ongaro, *Public Administration in Europe* (pp. 1–8).

Ongaro, E. (2020). Forms of Knowledge for the Practice of Public Administration. In Bouckaert and Jann, *European Perspectives for Public Administration* (pp. 273–282).

Owens, T. L. (2017). Higher Education in the Sustainable Development Goals Framework. *European Journal of Education*, 52(4), 414–420.

Pattyn, V., Broucker, B., & Brans, M. (2008). Quality Management in Public Administration Master Programs: Towards a Holistic Approach. In: Jenei Mike, *Public Administration and Public Policy Degree Programs in Europe* (pp: 81–105). NISPAcee Press, Slovak Republic.

Perales Franco, C., & McCowan, T. (2021). Rewiring Higher Education for the Sustainable Development Goals: The Case of the Intercultural University of Veracruz, Mexico. *Higher Education*, 81(1), 69–88.

Peterson, S. B. (2015). *Public Finance and Economic Growth in Developing Countries: Lessons from Ethiopia's Reforms*. London: Routledge.

Pham, H. T. (2018). Impacts of Higher Education Quality Accreditation: A Case Study in Vietnam. *Quality in Higher Education*, 24(2), 168–185.

Pinheiro, R., Šima, K., Young, M., & Kohoutek, J. (2018). University Complexity and Regional Development in the Periphery. In Pinheiro, R., Young, M., and Šima, K. (ed.) *Higher Education and Regional Development* (pp. 1–20). Cham: Palgrave Macmillan.

Randma-Liiv, T., Vintar, M., Proeller, I., & Profiroiu, M. C. (2019). EGPA and the European Administrative Space: Strategic Partnership with NISPAcee and the Trans-European Dialogue (TED). In: Ongaro, *Public Administration in Europe* (pp. 71–81).

Rosenbaum, A. (2015). International Accreditation, IASIA and the International Commission of Accreditation of Public Administration Education and Training Programs (ICAPA). In: Rosenbaum, (*In Quest for Excellence* (pp. 13–22).

Rugasira, A. (2013). *A Good African Story: How a Small Company Built a Global Coffee Brand*. Bodley Head, London.

Salto, D. J. (2018). Quality Assurance through Accreditation: When Resistance Meets Over-Compliance. *Higher Education Quarterly*, 72(2), 78–89.

Schwarz, S., & Westerheijden, D. (2004). Accreditation and Evaluation in the European Higher Education Area. https://eclass.upatras.gr/modules/document/file.php/PN1589/Accreditation%20and%20Evaluation%20in%20the%20EHEA.pdf#page=54.

Siffin, Wi. (2001). Problem of Development Administration. In: Farazmand, A. (ed.),*Handbook of Comparative and Development Public Administration* (2nded.). Marcel Dekker, New York.

Tadesse, T. (2014). Quality Assurance in Ethiopian Higher Education: Boon or Bandwagon in Light of Quality Improvement? *Journal of Higher Education in Africa/Revue de l'enseignement supérieur en Afrique*, 12(2), 131–157.

Tamrat, W. (2020). The Nuts and Bolts of Quality Assurance in Ethiopian Higher Education: Practices, Pitfalls, and Prospects. *Journal of Education Policy*, 1–18.

UN-ECA (2021). Seventh Session of the Africa Regional Forum on Sustainable Development: Summary, Key Messages and Brazzaville Declaration. ECA/RFSD/2021/15.

United Nations (2015). Transforming Our World: The 2030 Agenda for Sustainable Development. General Assembly (70/1).

REFERENCES

Useh, U. (2021). Sustainable Development Goals as a Framework for Postgraduate Future Research Following COVID-19 Pandemic: A New Norm for Developing Countries. *Higher Education for the Future*, 8(1), 123–132.

van der Krogt, T. (2015). Quality Standards and Public Administration Education and Training. In Rosenbaum., *In Quest of Excellence* (pp. 99–129).

Vaughan, S., & Gebremichael, M. (2011). *Rethinking Business and Politics in Ethiopia*. Africa Power and Politics, UK Aid, Irish Aid.

World Bank (2013). Federal Democratic Republic of Ethiopia Public Sector Reform Approach Building the Developmental State—A Review and Assessment of the Ethiopian Approach to Public Sector Reform, Report No: ACS3695, The World. http://documents.worldbank.org.

World Bank (2021). *Human Capital Index*. 2020 Update. https://documents.worldbank.org.

World Economic Forum. (2020). The Future of Jobs Report 2020. https://www.weforum.org/reports/the-future-of-jobs-report-2020/.

Zhou, L., Rudhumbu, N., Shumba, J., & Olumide, A. (2020). Role of Higher Education Institutions in the Implementation of Sustainable Development Goals. In: Nhamo & Mjimba, In *Sustainable Development Goals and Institutions of Higher Education* (pp. 87–96). Springer, Cham.

Useful Websites

Institution	website
African Association of Public Administration and Management (AAPAM)	https://www.aapam.org/
Ethiopian Higher Education Relevance and Quality Agency (HERQA)	https://herqa.edu.et/f
European Association for Public Administration Accreditation (EAPAA)	https://www.eapaa.eu/
European Public Administration Network (EPAN)	https://www.eupan.eu/
Harmonization of African Higher Education Quality Assurance and Accreditation (HAQAA)	https://haqaa2.obsglob.org/
International Commission on Accreditation of Public Administration Education and Training Programs (ICAPA)	https://iasia.iias-iisa.org/accreditation.php
International Institute of Administrative Sciences (IIAS)	https://iias-iisa.org/
National Association of Schools of Public Affairs and Administration (NASPAA)	https://www.naspaa.org/
Network of Asia Pacific Schools and Institutes of Public Administration and Governance (NAPSIPAG)	https://www.napsipag.org/cons_law.asp
Network of Schools and Institutes of Public Administration in Central and Eastern Europe (NISPAcee)	https://www.nispa.org/
United Nations Department of Economic and Social Affairs (UNDESA)	https://www.un.org/en/desa

www.ingramcontent.com/pod-product-compliance
Ingram Content Group UK Ltd.
Pitfield, Milton Keynes, MK11 3LW, UK
UKHW021834140426
5217IPUK00021B/1443